Introduction to Scheduling with Microsoft Project

Best Practices from Project MVPs

A manual by Advisicon®
Helping You Build a Project
Management Culture

5411 NE 107th Avenue, Suite 200
Vancouver, Washington 98662
Tel 360-314-6702

ADVISICON®

Identification and Notices

Publisher: Advisicon, Inc.
5411 NE 107th Avenue, Suite 200
Vancouver, Washington 98662

the accuracy of performance, compatibility, or any other claims related to these products. Questions on the capabilities of products should be addressed to the suppliers of those products.

This information contains examples used in daily business operations. To illustrate them as completely as possible, the examples may include the names of individuals, companies, brands, and products. All of these names are fictitious and any similarity to the names and addresses used by an actual business enterprise is entirely coincidental.

Case studies, exercises, and illustrations contained in this publication may include the names of individuals, companies, brands, and products. All of these names are fictitious and any similarity to the names used by an actual business enterprise is entirely coincidental.

Authors and Versions

The following individuals are recognized for their contributions to this work:

Author	Tim Runcie, MCP, MCTS, PMP, MVP
Author	Cindy Lewis, MOS, MCTS, MS, MCT, PMP, PMI-SP, MVP
Author	Ellen Lehnert, PMP, MVP, MCT, MCP
Editor, Designer	Jeff Jacobson-Swartfager
Editorial Coordinator	Pam Greensky
Contributor	Jesse Phillips-Mead, MCP

Version 2.00

ISBN: 978-1-60298-020-4

About Advisicon

Advisicon is a professional project and portfolio management consulting, training, and custom application development company. We help our clients leverage the best practices of project management methods and technologies to manage projects more effectively.

Advisicon is a Registered Education Provider (REP) of the Project Management Institute (PMI), giving clients the confidence that they have chosen an organization that is well qualified to provide the instruction they need as well as the convenience of receiving Professional Development Units (PDUs).

Advisicon is a Microsoft® Gold Certified Partner in Project and Portfolio Management, Silver Certified in Collaboration and Content, Silver Certified in Learning, and multiple other advanced certifications. Advisicon helps organizations use Microsoft Project, Microsoft Project Server and SharePoint Services to manage their projects more effectively through optimization, training in best practices, and process and template development. Advisicon's consultants deliver deep expertise to our clients to help them use Project more effectively to deliver sustained results.

Our People

Advisicon's team of professionals includes Project Management Institute certified Project Management Professionals (PMPs), Microsoft Certified Professionals with specializations in Enterprise Project Management, Networking and Infrastructure Solutions, and Microsoft MVPs.

Our Philosophy

Advisicon is about delivering: Optimization, Knowledge Transfer and Sustained Results.

Our Services

- Microsoft Project and Project Server deployments, consulting and training
- SharePoint deployment, custom WebPart development, and training
- Microsoft Access & SharePoint application development, consulting and training
- Project management office formation and development
- Project and portfolio management consulting and training
- Project management maturity assessments
- On-site project management support
- Custom application and database development

Our Team

- Project Management Institute-certified PMPs
- Microsoft® Certified Professionals (specializations in Enterprise Project Management, Networking and Infrastructure Solutions)

Advisicon serves clients in every type of industry including business, government, and non-profit. Our services span international companies in North, Central and South America as well as Europe and Asia Pacific.

Visit Advisicon's website to read case studies of how Advisicon has helped clients, or to learn more about our services and products, contact Advisicon at 1-866-36-ADVIS or visit us at www.Advisicon.com.

About the Authors

Tim Runcie, MCTS, MCP, PMP, MVP, Advisicon President

Tim Runcie, the President of Advisicon, has over 25 years of experience in Information Systems and 15 years in Construction Management. Tim has been recognized by Microsoft as an MVP (Most Valuable Professional) for his outstanding excellence in Office and for his support to technical communities worldwide. He was first recognized as an Access MVP and has continued to gain recognition as a Project Portfolio Manager (PPM) in Enterprise Project, Program and Portfolio Management MVP for his expertise in MS Project, Project Server & SharePoint. This award has to be renewed annually and is extremely competitive. Tim has held this for over 10 years.

Microsoft Partner
Project and Portfolio Management
Collaboration and Content
Learning

Tim has been assisting Project Management Offices and Organizations (PMO's) in leveraging technology like Office Applications, Project, Project Server & SharePoint to meet their business Intelligence and reporting needs. His experience covers all sectors of customer industries such as High Tech, Government, Non-Profit, Private Business, Manufacturing, Construction, Banking, Healthcare and the Information Services or Information Technology industries.

He has focused in consulting, mentoring and training organizations to successfully complete their projects using scarce re-sources, fixed budgets and interconnected schedules, while leveraging technologies to automate and create powerful visual reports. Tim combines industry best practices, a passion for knowledge transfer, and tools development to optimize Project and Project Portfolio Management processes and to successfully integrate Project Management best practices into organizations' culture.

Tim loves teaching. When not leading or mentoring organizations, he is teaching classes centered on the disciplines and technologies of Project Management. To every project he brings a personal passion for education and a commitment to providing Advisicon's customers with a full set of skills and tools to achieve optimum success.

Cindy M. Lewis, MCTS, MCITP, MCT, PMP, PMI-SP, MVP

Cindy is the Director of Knowledge Management at Advisicon, Inc. She brings over 20 years of experience in scheduling, training and managing large projects. As a professional project manager, Cindy has focused her career on Information Technology projects specializing in company-wide system implementations spanning industries such as architecture, financial, manufacturing, medical, education and high tech. Cindy has in-depth expertise in lifecycle management, organizational project/portfolio process development and management, and customized curriculum development and execution.

Cindy has been a sought-after consultant called on to help numerous companies both locally and across North America to deploy, assist and, if needed, rescue failed Project Server implementations in versions 2002, 2003, 2007, 2010, 2013, and Project Online. In Project Server Cindy has captured complex business requirements and delivered a best in case solution recommending features that derive value for the business and provided consultative training to apply these features immediately. She has deployed Project Server, deployed Proof-of-Concept instances and has directed Project Server upgrades. Her vast experience includes working with both on-site and cloud based (hosted) solutions.

Her passion is training and leading large groups via both live and virtual classrooms. Courses are delivered several times a month onsite at customer training facilities.

Cindy received the Most Valuable Professional (MVP) award in Project by Microsoft in 2012 and 2013. With an estimate of less than 60 people receiving this designation for Project out of the thousands of MVPs awarded worldwide, this is a great testament to her dedication to the scheduling community. She is the second person at Advisicon to receive this award following Tim Runcie. If you haven't seen Cindy, watch for her at the next Microsoft or PMI conference or event. Some of her past duties at these events included giving presentations, staffing hands-on labs, working Project kiosks and booths, demoing software, and working at Ask the Experts' events.

Ellen Lehnert, PMP, MVP, MCT, MCP

Ellen is a Consultant/Trainer/Implementator for MS Project/MS Project Server. With over 20 years of corporate training and consulting experience, Ellen has taught MS Project over 400 times. In addition to co-authoring this publication she is the author of "Managing Projects using MS Project 2010 desktop" courseware, a contributor and tech editor for many reference books, is a developer for the MS Project 2010 & 2013 certification tests, writes a column for the Microsoft Project User Group (MPUG) newsletter, is a board member Chicago MPUG, and is a frequent meeting speaker. She is the owner of LehnertCS, LLC consulting/training company, www. lehnertcs.com and can be reached at ellen@lehnertcs.com.

Comments & Feedback

We are interested in your feedback about this publication. It is our goal to continually improve our books and resources and to enhance your learning experience. Please email us at info@Advisicon.com, and let us know your thoughts.

We look forward to hearing from you. Happy learning!

Contents

How To Use This Book

Conventions Used in this Book

Legend of Icons

A number of icons are used in this book to highlight important information.

The PMBOK icon and call-out box refers you to where you can find a concept or term in the Project Management Institute's Project Management Body of Knowledge – The PMBOK.

The Note Icon and call-out box indicates a key fact or insight to help participants better understand helpful background information, quirks, explanations for the way things work, answers to Frequently Asked Questions (FAQs), and helpful things to remember.

The Tip, Trick and Shortcut icon and call-out box presents quick ways to do things faster and impress colleagues.

The Warning Icon and call-out box will draw your attention to important risks, pitfalls, potential issues, and alternate concepts that may assist you with managing your project processes.

The Meaning of the Fonts

This book uses a few conventions to display meaning within the text.

Bold text indicates the title of a button, menu item, or file name, that should be clicked on or selected to complete a step. Bold text also indicates a key word or phrase worthy of consideration.

Text that is set in a `monospace` font indicates text that needs to be typed in (like a URL, or code).

Navigating this Book

This book has been organized so that each chapter can build upon the concepts and skills learned in the previous chapters. However, each chapter is designed to be relatively self contained. Keep an eye out for any cross-references to find more information on a subject.

Chapter 1

Introduction to Project Management

"I often say that when you can measure what you are speaking about,
and express it in numbers, you
know something about it; but when
you cannot express it in numbers,
your knowledge is of a meagre and
unsatisfactory kind; it may be the
beginning of knowledge, but you
have scarcely, in your thoughts,
advanced to the stage of science,
whatever the matter may be."

~ William Thomson (Lord Kelvin)

Overview

Project management is a global discipline that follows methodologies (aka, "recipes") to provide advantages to an organization. Our *Introduction to Project Management* is a very small introduction. At Advisicon, we encourage all of our clients to do further reading or join a project management organization such as the Project Management Institute (PMI)®[1] to further their expertise in this area. You should do the same.

Project managers are often called upon to work as schedulers or to collaborate with others who perform the scheduling role. The practices in this book will ensure that individuals working in Microsoft Project 2013 and performing scheduling functions take advantage of the best features of Project. Before we take you through Project 2013, we will explore some of the project management concepts this book is based on.

---

1   PMI is a registered mark of the Project Management Institute.

Projects

Every organization has objectives to accomplish as part of doing business. Examples include creating marketing plans, developing products, gaining new customers, improving processes, and so on. When these company objectives are well defined and their results can be verified, a project is often created. A **project** consists of:

- A defined timeline including a start date and (often) a finish date target.
- A verifiable objective or goal that when accomplished signals the completion of the project.
- An application of company resources to help complete the project, such as a budget and resources.
- A dedicated manager to lead the project.

Projects are different from other company operations in that they are created for a specific objective and disbanded when that objective has been accomplished. Projects help focus organizational resources to accomplish an objective quickly and effectively.

When projects are discussed, they are often discussed in terms of the **constraints** on them. Project managers and schedulers have to negotiate for resources at specific points in time or negotiate for funding to purchase goods or services. The limitations on resources and funding are referred to as "constraints," and can alter the speed at which a project is accomplished.

Constraints vary from project to project. On some projects, one constraint may be very tight, but the rest can give. On other projects you may be dealing with several tight constraints.

Still, every project has multiple possible constraints. Most specific constraints fall into one of five constraint types: budget, resources, time, quality, and scope. The level of sway each constraint has over a project determine the project's shape.

Figure 1-1 shows the shape of a project with a very tight resources constraint. In order to remain a feasible project, the other constraints have to be able to give.

A tight constraint forces some constraints to give more than others. In *Figure 1-1*, the time and scope constraints must be flexible in order to prevent the major constraint (resources) and the secondary constraints (budget and quality) from sinking the project.

Figure 1-1   Illustration of Constraints on the Project.

A schedule is a model of a project. It describes the relationship of items needed to reach the project's goal. Schedules also help manage the relationships between tasks and resources. Good communication is a critical aspect of successful projects and schedules are usually the means to do that. The benefits of scheduling and a more detailed explanation of Project 2013 are covered in Chapter 2, *Overview of Microsoft Project*.

Programs

Projects may be grouped into programs. A **program** is a collection of projects that are managed together because there is a benefit of doing so. Organizations assign a "program manager" to oversee the collection of projects while still giving individual project managers the authority to manage the work specific to their own project.

To better understand the difference between a project and a program, consider a magazine publisher who issues a new magazine every month. Each issue is a project with a timeline, a goal, and a project manager. The overall publication year, which consists of 12 issues, is managed as a program. This can help ensure that lessons learned from the creation of each issue are applied to future issues. The program manager can save money by negotiating resources for all 12 issues (e.g. paper, printing, distribution, etc.). Running a program is a good way to ensure consistency and delivery of the issues is optimized.

Portfolios

If your organization participates in strategic goal setting and comes up with defined strategic objectives each year, portfolio management might be useful. Examples of strategic objectives include:

- Increasing market share
- Increasing repeat customer business
- Improving employee efficiency

A **strategic objective** is a goal for the entire company; one person and one project would not be enough to accomplish this goal. Your company may assign a portfolio manager to oversee several strategic objectives.

A **portfolio** consists of projects and programs which may or may not directly relate to each other, but which collectively support the strategic goal. A program which consists of projects focused on updating technology does not directly relate to a project which creates an employee cafeteria. However, managed as a portfolio, all of these projects support the strategic objective of improving employee efficiency.

For further reading on the topic of project management, refer to standards developed by PMI[2]. These standards provide generally accepted concepts and principles but do not discuss project management software. The Project Management Institute, *A Guide to the Project Management Body of Knowledge, (PMBOK® Guide) – Fifth Edition, Project Management Institute Inc, 2013* and *The Practice Standard for Scheduling – Second Edition*[3] are excellent compliments to this book.

---

2   PMI is a registered mark of the Project Management Institute.
3   PMBOK is a registered mark of the Project Management Institute.

Project Management Processes

Project 2013 can be used to help manage projects, programs, and portfolios. To help drive success, organizations implement project management processes and lifecycle approaches when creating schedules. We discuss lifecycles in Chapter 4, *Task Development*. A project management **process** is an approach that is standard across all schedules. It consists of high-level phases that are followed in an ordered pattern and phases may be repeated. An example of a process is:

1. Feasibility Study
2. Funding and Approval
3. Detailed Planning
4. Staffing
5. Execution and Delivery
6. Acceptance and Close-Out
7. Review and Analysis

Organizations use processes to ensure consistency and to train project managers and schedulers on business processes proven to successfully manage projects. Earlier phases can be repeated even if the project has moved onto later phases in the process. For example, it is feasible for 'funding and approval' to be repeated during 'execution and delivery' if an addition to the project requires additional funding for implementation. This will allow for an addition to the project to receive additional funding to help it be implemented.

If your organization does not have a project management process, we recommend you obtain a copy of the PMBOK® Guide and review the high-level process groups and the iterative nature of some of those groups. They are listed in order below for your convenience:

1. Initiating
2. Planning
3. Executing
4. Monitoring and Controlling
5. Closing

At Advisicon, we believe so strongly in the PMI recommendations that we are a Registered Education Provider for PMI. We will use PMI's process groups as the project management foundation for this book. If you would like more information about these groups, refer to our book *Practical Project Management*.

Project Server

Project is a software tool that can be part of an enterprise project or portfolio management system. Organizations looking for a portfolio management system may purchase and deploy Project Server. Advantages of Project Server include:

- Centralized resources in an enterprise resource pool provides insight into capacity across all projects.
- Consolidated project views in an online format provides information about schedule and budget status across all projects.
- User and group permissions enable a well-defined security approach to schedules by limiting access to portions of the schedule and limiting the ability to change information.
- Online access to project data provides the ability to use web browsers and handheld devices to view and update project information.
- Real-time information sharing and collaboration in an online format gives you the ability to make decisions using current and complete information.

Most features discussed in this book are also available in a Project Server environment. However, organizations have the option to implement security policies in Project Server which can eliminate or change the availability of features in Project.

The focus of this book is on Project desktop (Project Standard and Project Professional) features only. To use Project with Project Server, you have to ensure you have the appropriate version. Refer to *"Project Desktop 2013 Overview of Versions"* in Chapter 2, *Overview of Microsoft Project* for further details on features and versions. Project Server capabilities are discussed in our book, *Microsoft Project Server 2013: Project Manager's Guide*.

Key Points to Remember

We've provided some background on project management and gave you some information about how Project can support that need. We will dive further into the advantages of Project in Chapter 2, *Overview of Microsoft Project*.

- Project management is a discipline that can help an organization receive benefits from their projects.
- A project is created to accomplish a specific objective and it is limited by constraints.
- A program is a collection of projects which have a related goal.
- A portfolio is a collection of projects and programs which have a strategic objective.
- A project management process may be used to guide projects through phases in an organized, repeatable manner. Throughout the process, an individual phase may be repeated if needed.
- An organization that uses Project Server will gain benefits of an enterprise project management system such as consolidated resource capacity, real-time project information, and defined security policies.

Chapter 2

Overview of Microsoft Project

"The most human thing about
us is our technology."

~ Marshall McLuhan

Overview

Using Project as your scheduling software provides many advantages. Project functions as a database and supports relationships between tasks, resources and costs. The level of detail and features implemented in the schedule can vary by project. To be most successful, you should plan an approach and select the appropriate version to achieve your scheduling goals. No matter what version is selected, you will be able to use the standard interface features available in other Microsoft software, such as the Ribbon. Project has numerous views, shortcuts, and features to quickly display the information needed which can help drive decisions for the project. The software techniques demonstrated in our *Overview of Micro-soft Project* are critical to the effective use of Project. These techniques will form the foundation of your further learning about Project.

Benefits of Scheduling Software

Project is a scheduling software used to manage projects. The software is flexible to allow for a variety of uses for different industries and different project management processes, or methodologies. The concept of scheduling is the coordination of activities, resources, money, time, and other variables that factor into completing a list of tasks containing task and resource relationships. Often scheduling involves working with limitations and date goals that are driven by the organization.

Throughout this book, you will become familiar with features available in Microsoft Project 2013. Below is a list of some of those features:

1. The ability to plan and manage a project using a Work Breakdown Structure (outline) format
2. Work, duration and cost planning, forecasting and tracking
3. Flexible reporting capabilities and customization
4. Ability to integrate with Project Server
5. Manual and automatic project scheduling
6. Resource management planning and forecasting
7. Budget forecasting and tracking
8. Baseline and variance reporting
9. Schedule predictability and what-if scenarios
10. Dynamic schedule management

Scheduling software has a flow of activities which compliments an overall project management process in an organization. Refer to the following steps as an example of how this might be applied.

1. The project is defined and the decision is made to perform the project
2. More in-depth planning is conducted to elaborate the tasks, resources and work required to complete the project
3. The project work is initiated
4. Information about how the work is getting accomplished is fed back to the project manager and updated into the schedule
5. Stakeholders request a change to the project and the project manager updates the schedule as needed
6. Reports are produced to reflect project status and schedule

7. Steps 4-6 are repeated until the project is completed
8. When the project is completed a transition will be made to move the results of the project into ongoing business operations or business processes
9. Time is set aside to reflect on how the project was executed and opportunities for process improvement are collected.

Figure 2-1 shows an example of a possible scheduling flow of activities. In this example, notice that updates to the project schedule come both from the information gathered during the implementation of the project work and from changes requested by stakeholders. Sometimes stakeholders request a change after seeing a report, other times they request a change while watching the project progress unfold. All projects evolve as decisions are refined or new information is obtained by the project manager or scheduler.

Notice that completion of a project is not the end of the flow of activities. Many times the results of a project generate a new process for the business which must be maintained. For example, a project to install a new alarm system with access cards does not end after the system in installed. Someone needs to be assigned to configure cards for new employees, run system tests, and replace broken components. This would be considered ongoing operations in the diagram.

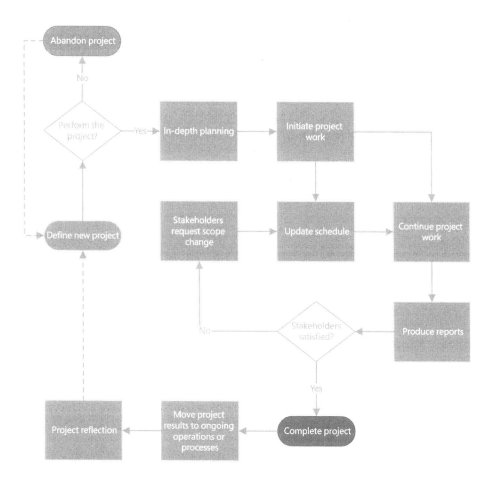

Figure 2-1   Scheduling software flow of activities.

Overview of Project as a Database

Although Project may in some ways look like Excel, it is actually a very complex database. Below are some reasons to use a database:

- Eliminates the need to have information duplicated in multiple locations
- Creates a structure of information that can be organized by subject
- Creates the ability to have information related to each other
- Simplifies the ability the report on related information crossing multiple subjects

If Project was set up like a single file is in Excel, each time you assigned a resource to a task, you would have to duplicate all the details about the resource on every single task. This would create a lot of unnecessary information. In addition, every time a resource detail was changed, this would have to be duplicated on every single task. Duplicate information is a good reason to use a database structure.

By using a database structure within Project, the resource is instead connected to a task but all the details about the resource are stored in another location. This way when a report is needed, details can be pulled from multiple locations. This book is not designed to teach everything that you need to know about databases but please refer to the following chart for an example of how all of this information works together.

Task Table

Unique ID	Task
1	Eat lunch
2	Mow lawn
3	Take out garbage
4	End world hunger

Resource Table

Unique ID	Resource
1	Pete
2	Jim
3	Sally

Assignment Table

Unique ID	Task	Resource
1	Eat lunch	Pete
2	Mow lawn	Jim
3	Take out garbage	Pete
4	Eat lunch	Jim

Figure 2-2   Illustration of Project Tables.

Notice that Project has three main tables of information – Task, Resource and Assignment. When a resource is assigned to a task, Project draws a connection/link between a unique resource field with a unique task field. Normally the unique field is not displayed in views, but can be added if desired.

Additional information about this database approach in Project:

- All the fields or columns of information are pre-defined when you create a project schedule. Creating a schedule is simply editing the information in fields/columns.

- Hiding a column in Project does not delete the information, it simply removes it from the current view
- Inserting a column is simply adding the information to a particular view
- Changing a field of information in one view is changing the information in the database and any other view that uses that field will display the change
- Some views are designed for a specific purpose and may display task information only, resource information only or some combination of task, resource, and assignment information. For example, the Resource Sheet view does not allow you to display task names in it. That is because it is a specific view to show resource details. If you want to see how those resources are assigned, you should consider another view such as Task Usage, Resource Usage, or Gantt Chart.

This brief discussion should start you on your way to learning more about Project and how its database structure works when managing schedules.

Project Usage

When working with information in Project, you can view data at a high-level or drill down to a detail level. Project offers timescaled views ranging from yearly all the way down to each minute. Schedulers, project managers, and other professionals using this tool will need to determine what level of information is needed to produce the desired output of information. You also need to determine how granular you want to be in maintaining that information.

For example, some organizations manage resource assignments by looking at the week as a whole and ensuring resources have 40 hours of work assigned to them. These organizations do not care if one day shows 6 hours and another day shows 12, they simply look at the total weekly hours. Other organizations drill into the daily view and ensure resources have 8 hours a day.

As you might realize, working with information drilled into the daily view will require you to manage tasks on a daily basis, while working with information on a weekly view only requires you to manage tasks on a weekly basis. This also drives the accuracy of your reports. Management of work on a daily basis gives you accurate reports for each day while management of work on a weekly basis only gives you accurate reports on a weekly basis.

When deciding your usage of project, keep in mind the following:

More Detail = More Work = More Results

Less Detail = Less Work = Less Results

Create a strategy for managing to a specific level of detail and stick with it to be most efficient in Project. For example – do not manage one task on a daily basis and another task on a weekly basis.

Formulate a Strategy

Before a project schedule is created, define what information you are hoping your schedule will return for the work and time you devote to using the schedule.

Set your goals for the project schedule:

1. Define the type of information your project schedule should return.
   a. When performing home remodeling you might be interested in when to schedule the contractors.
   b. When developing a software module you might be interested in estimating work hours of resources and costing.
   c. When performing annual maintenance of machinery you might be interested in the timeline and the number of resources needed to accomplish the project.
2. Different projects, by nature, require different levels of detail and tracking. Decide what is right for the project you need to accomplish. The more detail the more complex the schedule will become.
3. What type of metrics (field values i.e.: work, cost, duration, earned value, etc) will your project management and post-project reporting require?
4. How will you track your project?
5. What are your Stakeholders status reporting expectations? Define at the column level.
6. How much work are you as a project manager willing to do to achieve desired results?

If Project Managers preplan the requirements and the outputs of the project schedule, the schedule will be more productive and result in more valid data.

Project Managers have a tendency to make the project schedule become the project. Pre-planning will help project managers avoid this pitfall.

Success Checklist

Checklist to help plan a schedule more effectively:

1. **Goals**: Set the output goals of the schedule. Ask yourself: Management of the schedule is useful when I get what type of information from the schedule?
2. **Schedule**: Is the schedule a checklist of activities or is it tasks that will be managed? If it is a checklist, should it be an Excel list? If one task is late, should it change the dates for future related tasks?
3. **Reporting**: Request details of the content of status reporting required for the project from management. This will help in knowing which pieces of information you will need to focus on during schedule creation and management. It will also help set expectations for stakeholders.
4. **Data**: Gather requirements for data reports: by week? by department? by variance to baseline? etc. Some of this information will be standard in Project 2013 and some will be created using customization features.
5. **Tracking**: Are tasks required to be tracked by the number of hours worked per task or is tracking by percent complete sufficient? Defining the tracking of the project will be tied to the type of metrics that the project schedule will produce.
6. **Earned Value (EV)**: if measuring EV is a requirement, more task details, estimating, baseline and tracking details will be required. This will likely result in more work for the project manager. Is help available for managing the project schedule?
7. **Resources**: What kind of reporting requirements will resources be responsible for during the project and how will the data be used. Will resource availability be updated collected and updated to the project schedule?

Defining output requirements of the schedule will in turn define the benefits of creating and maintaining the schedule. Establishing these goals will help the project manager focus on the benefits of the schedule for each specific project.

Project Desktop 2013 Overview of Versions

Microsoft offers three different versions of Project

Project Standard – This is the base scheduling software product which provides functionality that supports a majority of individuals needing a robust schedule tool. Project Standard also provides the following:

- Integration with the Office Store so you can purchase Apps for Project 2013
- Integration with SkyDrive for cloud storage of your project plan

Project Professional – The version offers the same features as Project Standard but provides these additional functions:

- Ability to inactivate tasks for various business scenarios and to support agile project management
- Lync integration (2013 or later) to support team collaboration within Project
- Visual resource management using Team Planner view
- Ability to integrate with SharePoint 2013/SharePoint Online for storing of project plans and task syncing
- Ability to connect to Project Server 2013/Project Online to support an enterprise project and portfolio management system

Project Pro for Office 365 – The version offers the same features as Project Professional but provides these additional functions:

- Delivers the software as a subscription service so it is always up to date with updates to the software being applied on a regular basis through Office 365
- Provides the ability to stream software to up to 5 devices (e.g. home PC, work PC, and tablet) using a connected Office 365 account

Internet access will be required to have access to all of the functions listed above.

For a comparison of feature coverage between Project Professional, Project Professional for Office 365, Project Standard, PWA, and Project Lite, see *Project Feature Coverage* in the Appendix. Current pricing and a detailed comparison chart of features can be found at www.microsoft.com/project.

Review of the Ribbon, Back Stage View, Quick Launch

To take advantage of Project's many features, you need to be proficient in accessing schedule commands and file commands. In this section, we will review the organization of the Ribbon, when to access commands in Backstage view, and the benefits of the Quick Access toolbar.

Exploring the Ribbon

The Ribbon is the user interface which you will find across Microsoft products. Features are easy to find and there are new features available right at your fingertips. The series of tabs located at the top of the Ribbon represent the different sectors of work, such as resource management or task management. Starting with the Task tab, you will see it is divided into logical sections called groups. The group names are listed just below a collection of buttons. Buttons that are larger indicate a feature that is frequently used. Some of the important advantages to the Ribbon include:

- Everything is organized on tabs by subject area.
- Information on the Format tab automatically responds to the current working environment and provides "view" relevant buttons. Notice the view-specific heading above the Format tab.
- The size of the buttons adjust based on your available window or screen size so you don't lose any capabilities, while maintaining maximum screen real estate.
- Features are available in a quick one- or two-click fashion.
- You can tailor the Ribbon by adding and/or removing features or by adding a new tab.

The File tab is unique and will be addressed in the next section.

Figure 2-3   Microsoft Project 2013 Ribbon.

The Ribbon can be configured to auto-hide or auto-display giving you valuable screen space as you work on your schedule. To set this, click the "minimize the Ribbon" symbol in the upper right-hand corner of the screen.

Figure 2-4   Project Ribbon – Expanded.

To disable this feature, click the "Expand the Ribbon" symbol in the upper right-hand corner of the screen.

Figure 2-5   Project Ribbon – Minimized.

Backstage View (File Tab)

To centrally locate file management activities, they are located on the File tab. Think of what you "do to the entire file" when you enter this area. This area is now known as the Backstage view. Some of the features available include:

- New, open, save, print, share and export.
- Connect with SharePoint , Skydrive, Office 365, and Project Server/ Project Online.
- Project Options – aligning options to all new projects or only specific projects.

Figure 2-6   Backstage View (File Tab).

To exit Backstage View click the return arrow pointing left at the top of Backstage View.

Overview of Common Views

Project organizes views into two major categories: Task views and Resource views. A task view has a primary focus on showing task information while a resource view has a primary focus on showing resource information. Within those categories may be integrated views that showcase both task and resource information through resource assignments. This section is going to give you an introduction to common views that you should become familiar with to be successful in managing projects.

Task Views

Task views are accessed in a number of ways including through various tabs on the ribbon, through right-click short cuts and through the View Bar. You should find the option that you prefer.

Project lists 11 popular task views: Calendar, Detail Gantt, Gantt Chart, Gantt with Timeline, Milestone Rollup, Network Diagram, Task Form, Task Sheet, Task Usage, Timeline, Timeline, and Tracking Gantt. Some of these will be illustrated below.

To display a task view:

1. Click the **Task** tab.
2. Click the drop-down arrow on **Gantt Chart** in the View group.
3. Click the desired view.

Figure 2-7   Changing Views Icon.

Gantt Chart – the Gantt Chart is a graphic representation of the start and finish dates for a task. In addition to graphic bars, relationship arrows are also displayed. The advantage of the Gantt chart is it includes an Entry table on the left for easy data entry and it shows a graphical model on the right of the proposed plan for your project. This is the most popular view in Project.

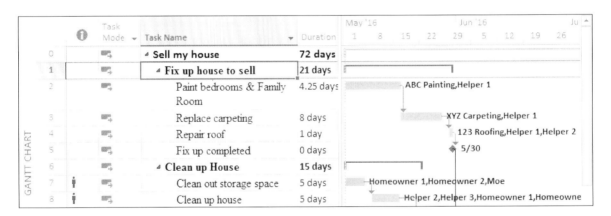

Figure 2-8   Gantt Chart View.

Tracking Gantt – this view will graphically represent the start and finish dates of a task like the Gantt Chart but is designed to help during the tracking phase of the project schedule. The advantage of this view is that the variance between the baseline plan and the current plan are shown visually.

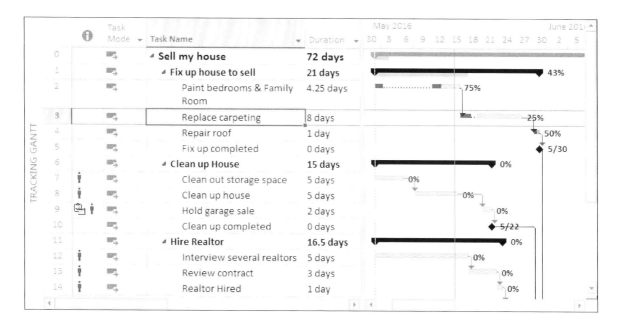

Figure 2-9   Tracking Gantt View.

Network Diagram – The Network diagram is designed as a precedence diagram. It shows the predecessors and successors of tasks without regard to timeframe. This view is useful to see the layout of your schedule to and easily follow links.

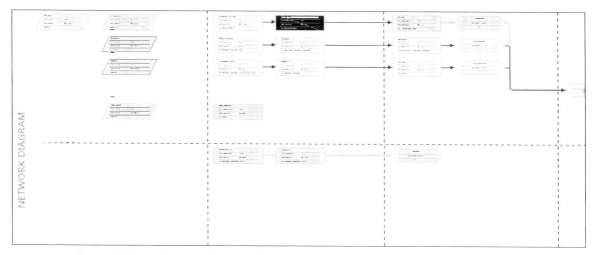

Figure 2-10   Network Diagram View.

Calendar view – The calendar view shows the project schedule in a calendar layout. This format is useful when presenting to individuals not familiar with how to read a Gantt Chart view.

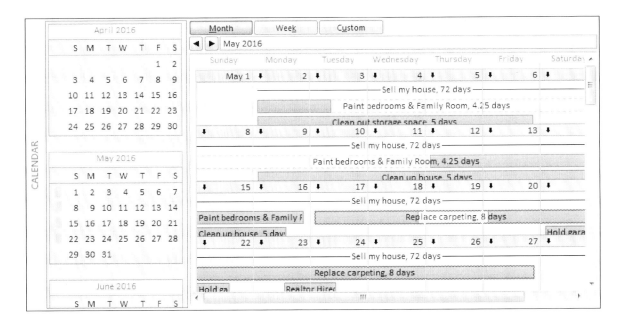

Figure 2-11   Calendar View.

Timeline View – The Timeline View is a very flexible and customizable view. Tasks may be selected to appear on the timeline to give high level reporting capability. In addition, the timeline has the ability to highlight the timeframe it is representing. The Timeline view will be discussed in Chapter 11, *Printing and Reporting*.

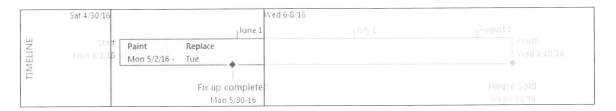

Figure 2-12   Timeline View.

Task Usage – The Task Usage view shows tasks and the resources assigned to the task. The advantage of this view is it includes resource assignments and shows numerically the resource needs to complete each task. Tailoring of this view provides cost or other fields of information.

	①	Task Mode ▾	Task Name ▾	Work ▾	Duratic ▾	Details	T	W	T	F	S
0		◼➚	◢ **Sell my house**	**2,492 hrs**	**72 days**	Work	68h	44h	24h	24h	
1		◼➚	◢ **Fix up house to se**	**132 hrs**	**21 days**	Work	4h	0h	0h	0h	
2		◼➚	◢ Paint bedrooms	68 hrs	4.25 days	Work	4h	0h	0h	0h	
			ABC Paintin	34 hrs		Work	2h	0h	0h	0h	
			Helper 1	34 hrs		Work	2h	0h	0h	0h	
3		◼➚	◢ Replace carpeti	40 hrs	8 days	Work					
			XYZ Carpetii	20 hrs		Work					
			Helper 1	20 hrs		Work					
4		◼➚	◢ Repair roof	24 hrs	1 day	Work					
			123 Roofing	8 hrs		Work					

Figure 2-13   Task Usage View.

Resource Views

Resource views are accessed in a number of ways including through various tabs on the ribbon, through right-click short cuts and through the View Bar. You should find the option that you prefer.

Project lists 5 popular resource views: Resource Form, Resource Graph, Resource Sheet, Resource Usage, and Team Planner. Some of these will be illustrated below.

To display a resource view:

1. Click the **Task** tab.
2. Click the drop-down arrow on **Gantt Chart** in the View group.
3. Click the desired view.

Figure 2-14   Changing Views Icon.

Resource Sheet – The resource sheet provides the table where resources are added into Project. The advantage of this view is the most popular fields needed to describe a resource are located here.

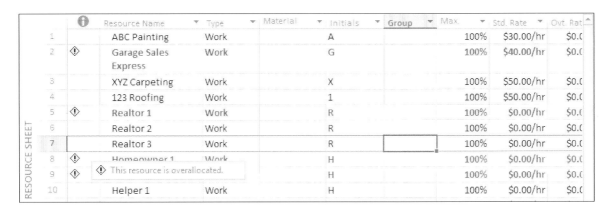

			Resource Name	Type	Material	Initials	Group	Max	Std. Rate	Ovt. Rate
1			ABC Painting	Work		A		100%	$30.00/hr	$0.0
2	◇		Garage Sales Express	Work		G		100%	$40.00/hr	$0.0
3			XYZ Carpeting	Work		X		100%	$50.00/hr	$0.0
4			123 Roofing	Work		1		100%	$50.00/hr	$0.0
5	◇		Realtor 1	Work		R		100%	$0.00/hr	$0.0
6			Realtor 2	Work		R		100%	$0.00/hr	$0.0
7			Realtor 3	Work		R		100%	$0.00/hr	$0.0
8	◇		Homeowner 1	Work		H		100%	$0.00/hr	$0.0
9	◇	◇ This resource is overallocated.				H		100%	$0.00/hr	$0.0
10			Helper 1	Work		H		100%	$0.00/hr	$0.0

Figure 2-15   Resource Sheet View.

Resource Graph – The Resource Graph graphically displays information about each resource. The advantage of this view is it can easily identify visually where a resource might be overallocated and by how much based on the length of the bar above the units available line (the darker horizontal line at 100% in *Figure 2-16*).

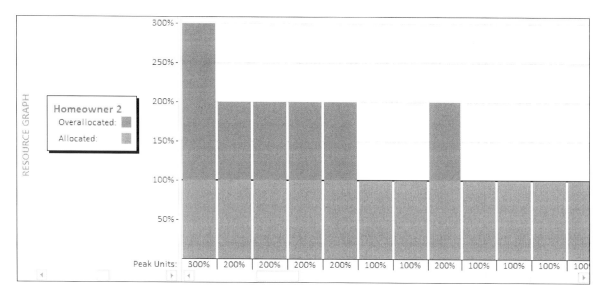

Figure 2-16   Resource Graph View.

Team Planner – the Team Planner view is a resource focused view that showcases work assignments in a graphical timeline format. The advantage of this view is that the focus is on the resource and graphically what work is scheduled at what time.

This feature is only available in Project Professional or Project Pro for Office 365.

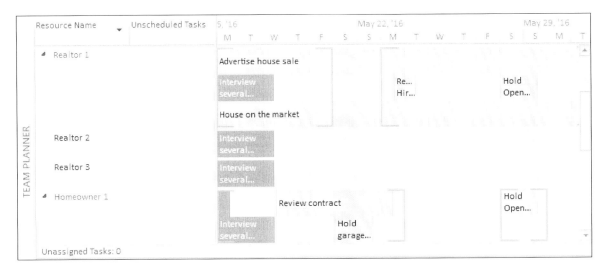

Figure 2-17   Team Planner View.

Resource Usage– The Resource Usage view shows every resource on the project and what tasks they have been assigned. The advantage of this view is it shows hours scheduled to accomplish each task. This view is a reversal of Task Usage view. Both of these views are useful in team meetings.

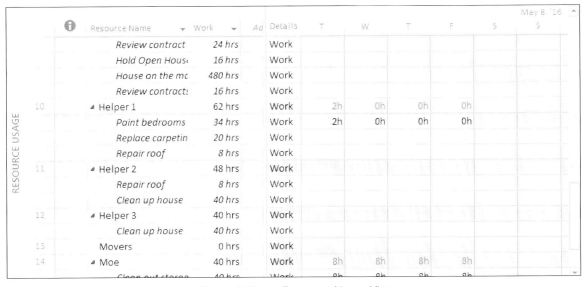

Figure 2-18   Resource Usage View.

Popular View Adjustments and Navigation

The most proficient schedulers and project managers jump through schedules very quickly to access the information they need. In this section, we will explore shortcuts to change the level of detail, display additional fields of information, jump quickly throughout Gantt chart view and shortcuts to locate a task.

Zooming In and Out

Zooming in or out is the way to adjust the bar chart or timescale portion of a view to show more or less detail. For example, you can display Gantt bars across a daily timescale or across a quarterly timescale.

Two popular methods for zooming in and out are using the Zoom Slider and the Zoom options on the View tab. The Zoom Slider is recommended since that option is always displayed even when you navigate to another view.

- You can click the minus and plus buttons to zoom out and zoom in.
- You can drag the zoom indicator in between the zoom out and zoom in buttons.

Figure 2-19   Zoom Slider.

Hide or Insert a Column

When you hide a column in Project 2013, the column is only removed from view, not deleted from your schedule. Keep in mind that hiding a column doesn't remove any information from your schedule.

Hide a Column

To hide a column from a sheet view:

1. In a sheet view, select the column you want to hide by clicking its title.
2. This displays the **Gantt Chart Tools** tab with the **Format** tab underneath in the Ribbon.
3. Click the **Format** tab.
4. Click the drop-down arrow on **Column Settings** in the Columns group.
5. Click **Hide Column**.

You can also press the **delete** key on your keyboard.

Figure 2-20   Column Adjustment Icons.

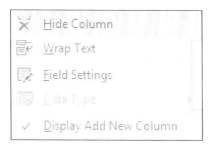

Figure 2-21   Column Settings Drop-down Menu.

Insert a Column

To insert or add a column:

1. In a sheet view, select the column to the right of where you want to insert the column.
2. This displays the **Gantt Chart Tools** tab with the **Format** tab underneath in the Ribbon.
3. Click the **Format** tab.
4. Click **Insert Column** in the Columns group.
5. A new blank column is displayed to the left of the column that you had selected. Click the drop-down arrow in the title box to specify the type of information from the list of possible column types (or fields) that the column will contain.

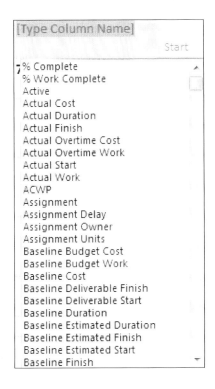

Figure 2-22   Add New Column.

Also at the end of every table in a Sheet view (the far right) there is an **Add New Column** option available.

Figure 2-23   Add New Column in View.

To unhide a previously hidden column, insert the column as you would with any new column.

Using the Scroll to Task Button

The Scroll to Task is a shortcut feature to bring information to you quickly. It is useful in views like Gantt Chart, Task Usage, and Resource Usage where there is a table of information on the left and an associated timescale of information on the right. The main advantage of this feature is to reduce time spent scrolling or looking for information.

To use Scroll to Task:

1. Click the task name or row ID number.
2. Click the **Task** tab.

3. Click **Scroll to Task** in the Editing group.

Figure 2-24   Scroll to Task Icon.

Project displays the date or dates where the selected task occurs on the timeline.

Go To and Find

As schedules begin to get larger, it is useful to have shortcuts to navigate through the information. In this topic, we will illustrate the advantages of Go To and Find within Gantt Chart view.

To Go To information:

1. Press the F5 key or Ctrl + G.
2. In the Go To dialog box, enter a row ID number or choose or enter the date and click **OK**.

To Find information:

1. Click the **Task** tab.
2. Click **Find** in the Editing group.
3. In the **Find** dialog box, enter or set the desired options and click **Find Next**.

Keyboard Shortcuts

Key Tips allow you to use your keyboard to navigate through the Quick Access Toolbar and the Ribbon. To turn on Key Tips, simply tap the Alt key. You can also press F10 twice. Follow the letters and numbers that are displayed to use the function you desire.

You can also use keyboard shortcuts to navigate through your project. The following table lists keys that are useful when navigating within views and windows.

Table 2.1   Key Tips and Keyboard Shortcuts

Key Tips & Shortcut	Outcome
Tab	Move right one field in an Entry table or dialog box.
Shift+Tab	Moves left one field in an Entry table or dialog box.
Home	Moves to the beginning of a row or field of information.
End	Moves to the end of a row or field of information.
Page Up	Moves up one screen.
Page Down	Moves down one screen.
Alt + Page Up / Alt + Page Down	Moves left or right one screen on the time scale.

Table 2.1   Key Tips and Keyboard Shortcuts

Key Tips & Shortcut	Outcome
Alt + ⇦ / Alt + ⇨	Moves the time scale one unit left or right (as defined by the bottom time scale tier).
Alt + Home	Moves to the project start date in the bar chart.
Alt + End	Moves to the project finish date in the bar chart.
Ctrl + Home	Moves to the first field in the first row of the Entry table or the same location in any other sheet view.
Ctrl + End, Home	Moves to the first field in the last row of the Entry table or the same location in any other sheet view.
Ctrl + ⇧	Moves to the First Row.
Ctrl + ⇩	Moves to the Last Row.
F1	Turns on Project Help.
F2	Activates in-cell editing for the selected field.
F3	Displays all tasks or resources when a prior filter was applied.
F5	Goes to a specific row ID number or a date on the time scale.
F6	Activates the other pane in a combination or dual-pane view.

Table 2.1   Key Tips and Keyboard Shortcuts

Key Tips & Shortcut	Outcome
F10	Press twice to turns on Key Tips. You can also tap the Alt key.
Ctrl + Shift + F5	Displays the Gantt bar for the selected task.
Ctrl + F4	Closes the Project window.
Ctrl + F5	Changes the Gantt Chart view from maximized to previous size (i.e., view window is separated from Project window).
Ctrl + F10	Maximizes the Gantt Chart view and combines it with the Project window.
Ctrl + F9	Allows you to turn on and off Auto Calculate.
Ctrl + F6	Displays the next open Project window.
Ctrl + Shift + F6	Displays the previous open Project window.
Alt + Spacebar / Alt + Hyphen	Displays the application control menu.
Insert	When the Task ID is selected, a new blank row is added in the Entry table.
Delete	When the Task ID is selected, a row is deleted from the Entry table.
Alt + F3	Displays the Field Settings dialog box for the active column.

Table 2.1   Key Tips and Keyboard Shortcuts

Key Tips & Shortcut	Outcome
Alt + F4	Closes Project.
Shift + F2	Displays Task Information in Gantt Chart view. Displays Resource Information in Resource Sheet view.
Shift + F3	Sorts by ID number.
Shift + F6	Enables the horizontal and vertical split bars in Gantt Chart view.
Shift + F11 / Alt + Shift + F1	Creates a new version of your schedule (e.g., Project: 2).

Help

Within Project, there are easy options to get help on features and functions. The default setting of the Ribbon provides detailed feature descriptions when you pause on a button. Should you need more assistance, a detailed help search is recommended.

The detailed help feature automatically assumes you are connected online, but you have the option to switch it to search on your computer only.

Navigation through help is just like a website and you will notice the home button, back button, and hyperlinks as being familiar to you.

To access Help:

1. Press the F1 key or click the help icon in the top right-corner (question mark).
2. Click the drop-down arrow on **Project Help** and choose the desired help option (online or not).
3. Enter the terms you want to search on in the text box and press the Enter key or magnifier icon.

Key Points to Remember

- Scheduling software offers benefits for managing budgets, resources, and tasks.
- Project is a database and offers many advantages; most importantly elimination of duplicate data entry.
- Determine the level of detail that is important to you before creating a schedule to provide a guideline for task development.
- Formulating a strategy and following a success checklist will help you get the most out of your Project schedule.
- Project Professional 2013 and Project Pro for Office 365 have essentially the same features, but the Office 365 version is available as a monthly subscription.
- Use Backstage view to make changes that alter the schedule file as a whole (e.g. header).
- Use the Ribbon to make changes within a schedule file by topic area (e.g. resources).
- Use the Quick Access toolbar for features that you always want available (e.g. undo).
- Views are illustrations of information in your Project database and all data is dynamically connected no matter what view you make a change in.
- Columns are fields in the database and you may show or hide them as needed. They are never permanently removed.
- Use the Scroll to Task feature to quickly display timeline details for a specific task and eliminate unnecessary scrolling.
- Keytips and keyboard shortcuts are alternative ways to navigate throughout Project without using the mouse.

ADVISICON®

Chapter 3
Start a Project

"Do not wait; the time will never
be 'just right.' Start where you
stand, and work with whatever
tools you may have at your
command, and better tools will
be found as you go along."

~ Napoleon Hill

Overview

New schedules can be created a number of ways: importing a task list, applying a template, or pulling data from Excel or SharePoint. Common tasks in managing existing schedule files include opening, saving, and exporting data. Project has many time-saving features that can be applied to help meet the needs of individuals who integrate with SharePoint or Excel.

After a schedule is up and running, next steps typically include configuring the standard calendar and setting project options (which may encompass Project globally or may apply only to an individual schedule). Scheduling options could have a dramatic impact on how tasks are calculated and those options should be evaluated before building a schedule.

Creating New Projects

One of the very first things you need to do to create a project is to choose an approach.

There are several methods to select from when creating a new schedule using Microsoft Project 2013. You may start a project schedule with a blank template or use an existing template. If you have a task list started in Excel, Outlook, Word and SharePoint, these task lists may be added to a new project schedule. Below are some of the suggested methods for initiating a new project schedule.

- Blank – clean schedule
- New From Existing – copy from existing schedule
- New From Excel – importing information from Excel
- New From SharePoint Tasks List – shortcut to bring SharePoint tasks into your schedule
- Get Started Wizard – guided approach with visuals to help individuals feel more comfortable working in a schedule
- Template – public or private pre-built schedules that can be used as examples

If you do not have Internet access, you may not have all of these choices. Many templates are available from the Microsoft site and are not included with the software when installed.

Office 365 or cloud users may have different choices depending on their organization's configuration.

To start a new project schedule:

1. Click the **File** tab.
2. Click **New**.
3. Click the desired item from the previews.

4. If needed, click **Create** to obtain a copy of that item to start your schedule.

Templates available are simply examples and may not map to your organization's project management practices. Be sure to review the templates for modifications that you might need to make.

Saving a project

Saving a project is all about storing a project for quick and easy retrieval. You may choose to store your project on your computer, on a network location, or on a cloud storage solution. As each organization's configuration is different, we will focus on the procedures for saving to your local computer.

To save a new project:

1. Click the **File** tab.
2. Click **Save** or **Save As**.
3. Click **Computer**.
4. Click **Browse**.
5. Navigate to the desired folder.
6. Enter the desired name for the schedule.
7. Click **Save**.

> The folder you just used will be available under **Open, Computer** to simplify this process for future new projects.

> When making changes to the same project, you can use the **Save** icon on the Quick Access Toolbar as a fast method to ensure your project changes are being captures.

Save or Save As, Share and Export

When saving, there are different techniques that can be applied depending on whether the information is being saved for future use in Project or whether it will be used in another program such as Excel or SharePoint. The Save As option is also useful when a copy of the schedule is required for running a scenario or making a backup.

Saving the Schedule

Project 2013 provides multiple file formats for a project schedule. The steps to save a file are very similar to other Microsoft Office files.

To save the Project 2013 schedule:

1. Click **File** → **Save as** → select file location
2. Enter the file name in the File Name area
3. Click **Save** to complete the save. The file will be given a Project 2013 default file extension of .mpp

There is also an option to save the Project 2013 schedule in an alternative file format. Some of the formats are:

- Microsoft Project 2007
- Microsoft Project 2000-2003
- Microsoft Project template 2013 (*.mpt)
- Microsoft Project template 2007 (*.mpt)
- Microsoft Excel
- PDF Files (*.pdf)
- XPS Files (*.xps)
- XML Format (*.xml)
- CSV (Comma delimited) (*.csv)
- Text (Tab Delimited) (*.txt)
- Excel Workbook (*.slsx)
- Excel Binary Workbook (*.slsb)
- Excel 97-2003 (.xls)

Save As

The Save As view, located in the backstage area in Project 2013, has been enhanced and provides more functionality for the user. From the backstage view these options are an easy method of saving projects to disk as well as sharing projects schedules with others users. Options have been added to sync a project with a Sharepoint site and to save a project to a Skydrive site.

To navigate to the options available for Save As:

Click **File** → **Save As** → select one of the options offered

The right side of the screen will change as options are selected

Table 3.1 provides an explanation of the save as options available.

Table 3.1   Save Options from the File Tab

Share Option	Feature
Sync with Sharepoint Site	Sync task list to an existing or new Sharepoint site
[YOUR USERNAME]'s Skydrive	Save file to your Skydrive or a site you have access to
Computer	Save file to a location on your hard drive, a list of recently used locations will be displayed
Add a Place	Add other locations such as Cloud or Office 365

Table 3.2 provides a description of the share options available.

Table 3.2   Share Options from the File Tab

Share Option	Feature
Sync with Sharepoint Site	Sync task list to an existing or new Sharepoint site
Email	Will send the currently opened MS Project file as an attachment in an email

Table 3.3 provides a description of the export options available.

Table 3.3   Export Options from the File Tab

Export	Feature
Create PDF/XPS Document	A PDF of the current view will be created and saved to disk
Save Project as File	This feature will allow for: • Saving into earlier version formats of MS Project files • Saving templates • Saving data to Excel, XML or another type format. This option will also start the MS Project Export Wizard where data for exporting may be selected.

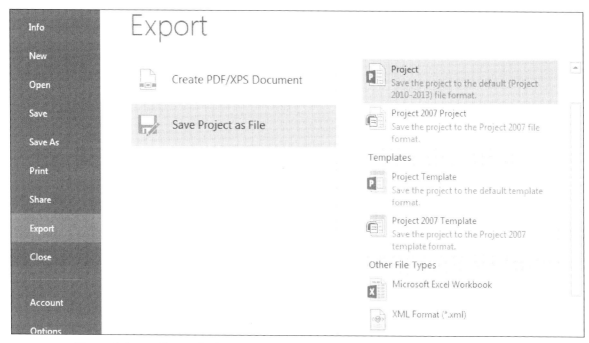

Figure 3-1   Export Project.

To email the current open file as an attachment in an email:

- Click on **File → Share → Email → Send as Attachment**

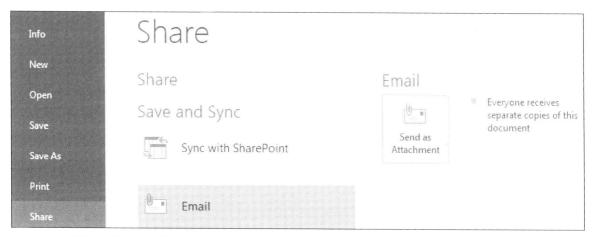

Figure 3-2   Share Email.

Microsoft Outlook will open with the file as an attachment. Select the email address, complete the email information and click **Send**.

Opening a Project

Since opening projects is such a frequent task, you should take advantage of quick methods to do this. The following steps will help you optimize your environment for speedy retrieval of projects.

To open a project:

1. Click the **File** tab.
2. Click **Open**.
3. Click **Computer**.
4. Click **Browse**.
5. Navigate to the desired folder.
6. Select the name for the schedule.
7. Click **Open**.

Click **Recent Projects** to quickly retrieve a project you have previously opened.

Pin a project to the top of the recent project list if you anticipate you will be using it on a regular basis.

Adding the **Open** button to the Quick Launch bar will save time.

Creating a New Project

When Project 2013 is initiated, a new blank project schedule will automatically appear.

To create a blank project schedule:

- Click **File → New**

Backstage choices shown below will give you an array of choices of where to begin a new project schedule. As you click the various choices, options and additional data will appear on the right side of the view.

- Clicking **Blank project** will result in creating a blank project file.
- **Recent Templates**: Create a project from a recently used template.
- **My templates**: Templates created by you and saved to your desktop.
- **New from an existing project**: Use an existing project schedule to create a new project.
- **New project from Excel workbook**: Columns in the Excel workbook will be mapped to fields within Project 2013. The import process is discussed in the next lesson.
- **New from Sharepoint task list**: Project 2013 Professional only. Tasks will be imported using the URL and security of the Sharepoint site.
- **Office.com templates**: Create a new project from a template that would be downloaded from Office.com online.

> If the Quick Access Bar was customized to add the **New** button, pressing that button will create a new project schedule

Figure 3-3   View for selecting how to create a new project.

Creating a Project from an Excel Workbook

A project schedule can be created using an Excel Workbook task list. Keep in mind that the fields or columns that are being imported from Excel will be mapped to fields or columns within Project 2013. Pre-planning to know which Excel fields should be mapped to which Project 2013 fields would be helpful.

To create a project schedule from an Excel Workbook:

1. Click **File → New → New From Excel Workbook**.
2. Navigate to the Excel file that contains the tasks to be imported into the schedule, click **Open**.
3. Project 2013 Import Wizard will start running – Click **Next**.
4. Select whether to use a new map that will be created or an existing Project import map. For this example we will create a new map. Click the radio button next to **New Map** and click **Next**.
5. Import can start a new project file, append to the end of an existing project file or merge the data using a merge field. In this example we will create a new project schedule. Click **As a new project** and click **Next**.
6. When the data is brought into Project 2013, select if the data is to be mapped to the Task fields, Resource fields or Assignment fields. Click **Tasks**.
7. If the originating Excel file contains header or title information, click **Import includes Headers**. The system will remove this row (the first line only) as the header row. Click **Next**.
8. The Task Mapping form will be used to view some of the data and map which Excel fields will be imported into which Project 2013 fields. Pull down the values in the **Select worksheet name option** and select the sheet name in Excel that contains the data to be imported. After the choice has been made, the data from the sheet will be available for viewing.
9. In the example below, the duration field from the Excel Workbook was able to be automatically mapped to the duration field in Project 2013. However, the Task Name field could not find a match. The correct field name for the task name field in Project 2013 is "Name". Click the red error message (not mapped) and select the field name of **Name**. Repeat for other fields to be imported. Not all fields are required during the import process which allows the user to pick and choose which ones are appropriate to the schedule. Click **Next** to continue after all columns have been mapped.

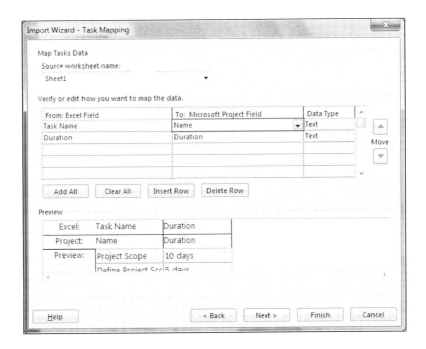

Figure 3-4   Mapping that is created in the Import Wizard.

10. The next step offers the option to save the map for future use.
    a. To skip saving the map, click **Next**.
    b. To save the map, click **Save Map** and give the map a name.
       Click **Finish** to start the import.
11. The new Project 2013 schedule will open with the columns imported.

Creating a Project from a SharePoint Task List

Project 2013 Professional allows for creating a new project by importing a task list from a SharePoint site. The user must have appropriate permissions to the access the SharePoint site and the URL path to insert into the form directing Project 2013 Pro to the location of the task list.

To import tasks from a SharePoint task list into Project 2013 Professional:

1. Click **File** → **New** → **New** from SharePoint Task List.

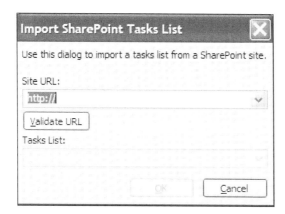

Figure 3-5   Enter the URL for the existing SharePoint site that contains a task list to import into the open project schedule.

2. Enter the URL in the form as shown above and click **Change to Check Address**. A list of all the task lists included in the SharePoint site will be displayed. Select the appropriate list and click **OK**.

The list will be imported from the SharePoint site.

This feature is available in Project 2013 Professional version only.

Calendar Overview

Calendars in Project 2013 will determine when a task may be scheduled within the project schedule. It will also influence what defines a day, a week and a month within the project schedule. The calendars will also work hand-in-hand with the calendar options to determine when and how the tasks will be scheduled. Having the correct calendar applied to the project schedule before tasks are entered is essential for project scheduling success.

We will explore:

1. How calendars work in Project 2013
2. How to Set Working Hours and Days
3. How to Set Non-Working Hours and Days
4. How to Set Calendar Options

How Calendars Work in Project 2013?

There are several types of calendars within the Project 2013 system. The following are definitions of available calendars:

- **Project Calendar**: The project calendar is the calendar assigned to a project and it defines the project working and non-working days. The default name for the Project Calendar is "Standard".
- **Resource Calendar**: Each resource will have its own calendar which may be based off of a base calendar or the project calendar. Unique resource calendars may also be created.
- **Task Calendar**: A task calendar is assigned to a task to allow for the scheduling of that task in a unique timeframe. For example: tasks which have to occur on a weekend.

A task will be scheduled based on the Project calendar until a resource is assigned to the task. At that time, the Resource calendar will control the scheduling of the task. Unless – there is a task calendar assigned to a task which will override the Project calendar and the Resource calendar.

When a project schedule is created, a default calendar of "Standard" is applied to the schedule. This is called the Project Calendar for the project. The default values on the Standard calendar are: Monday through Friday which are working days, and working time is 8:00 am to 12:00 pm and 1:00 pm to 5:00 pm daily. No holidays are indicated on the calendar. The Standard calendar is also the calendar that will be viewed in the background of the Gantt Chart view. The Calendar Options work hand in hand with the Project Calendar to determine number of hours in a day or week and these values should be in sync with one another. The Calendar options will be discussed in the next section.

By default, 2 additional calendars are included with MS Project 2013: a 24 hour calendar and a Night Shift calendar. Either of these may be used as Project, Resource or Task calendars.

FAQ's

Q: Why are there no holidays on the calendars?

A: This is an international program. Holidays vary from country to country.

Q: Is there the ability to add holidays to a calendar the way they can be added in Outlook?

A: No – this is not a capability of the software.

Q: Do I have to recreate the calendar for each project?

A: No – calendars may be created and saved through the Organizer to be used in future projects. The Organizer will be covered later in this chapter.

The default calendar name for the system is "Standard". If a
different calendar name is selected, the Gantt Chart view will
also require changing because the calendar which is displayed
is set to Standard. This change can be made by right clicking
in the Gantt view, selecting Non-working time and changing to
the desired calendar. Most users keep the Standard calendar
because of ease of use.

Setting Working Hours and Days

After the project file has been created, decide what the working days
(business days) of the project schedule will be. Decide also, how many
hours will make up a working day and what times the hours will be. By
default, the working days of the calendar are Monday through Friday and
the working time is 8:00 am to 12:00 pm and 1:00 pm to 5:00 pm daily or 8
hours working per day.

To Change the Working Hours of all Days on a Calendar:

1. Click **Project → Change Working Time**
2. Check to ensure the calendar you wish to change is displayed in the
   For calendar list
3. Click **Work Weeks** near the bottom of the dialogue box

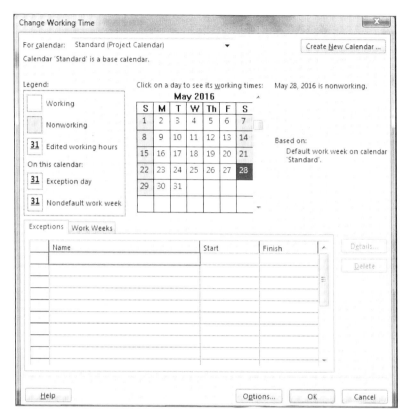

Figure 3-6   Change working time box used to change the working time of a selected calendar.

1. After clicking on the **Work Weeks** tab, the word Default should be highlighted. Click the **Details** button to the right of the dialog box.
2. Click **Monday**, press and hold the `shift` key and click on **Friday**. All of the working days will be selected.
3. Click the 3rd radio button, **Set day(s) to these specific working times**.
4. You will see the standard working times. Make changes to reflect the new values.
5. Click `Enter` or `Tab` to move away from the value you have changed.
6. Click **OK** to close the dialog box.

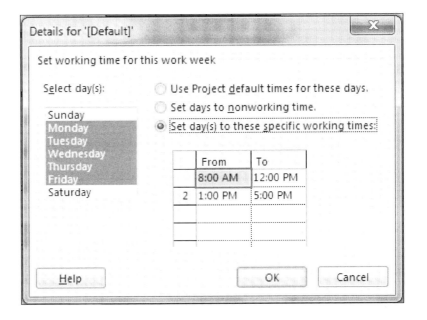

Figure 3-7   Change the time details of a selected day or group of days.

Military time is valid when entering hour values. To change 5:00 pm to 4:00 pm to shorten the work day, simply enter 16 where 5:00 pm is located and click Enter or Tab and 4:00 pm will appear.

Setting Non-Working Hours and Days

Non-working time is defined in the MS Project 2013 as days where work will not be planned or performed. Examples are: national and organizational holidays, training days, company shut-downs, summer hours, etc. Adding these non-working days and times to the project calendar will prevent tasks being scheduled on these non-working days.

To create a non-working day for a calendar:

1. Click **Project → Change Working Time**
2. Check to ensure sure that the calendar you wish to change is displayed in the **For Calendar** field
3. Click **Exceptions** tab near the bottom of the dialogue box

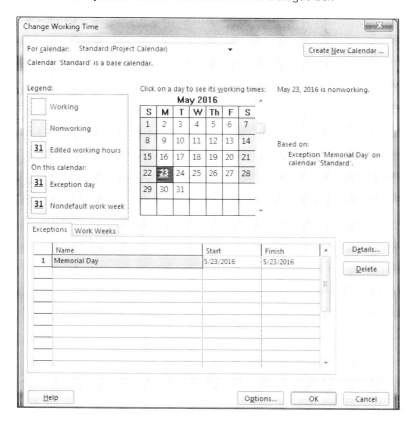

Figure 3-8   The Exceptions list is used to enter holidays or days that will be non-working days for the project.

4. In this example, we will set May 23, 2016 as a non-working day. Move the slider on the right side of the calendar down until **April 2016** is displayed in the calendar
5. Click **May 23, 2016**
6. Click in the name field and enter a reason for the non-working day, i.e.: Company holiday
7. Click Enter
8. Repeat for additional non-working days. See the result below

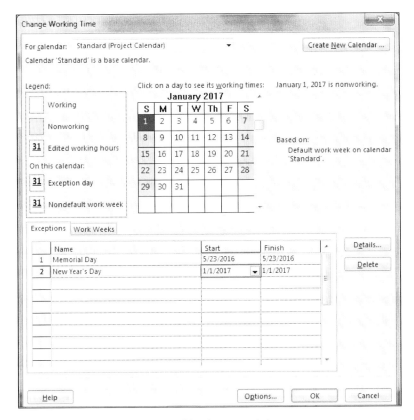

Figure 3-9   Change the working hours and days.

To Create a Recurring Non-working Day for a Calendar:

1. Click **Project → Change Working Time**
2. Check to make sure that the calendar you wish to change is showing in the **For calendar** field
3. Click the **Exceptions** tab near the bottom of the dialog box
4. In this example, we will set January 1 (New Year's Day) as a recurring non-working day. Move the slider on the right side of the calendar down until **January 2017** is displayed on the calendar
5. Click **January 1, 2017**
6. Click in the first open line in the **Name** field and enter **New Year's Day** for the non-working day
7. Click Enter
8. Click on the words **New Year's Day** and then click on the **Details** button to the right of the form

9. Click **Yearly**

10. Click on January 1

11. Enter the start date

12. Enter a recurrence value or an End by date

13. Click **OK** to close box

14. Check for the recurrence values in the Exceptions line for New Year's Day.

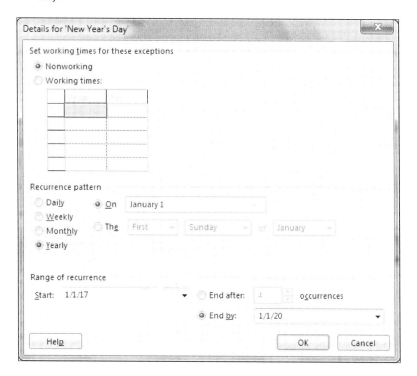

Figure 3-10   Recurring holiday values on calendar.

Setting Calendar Options

The Calendar options work hand in hand with the project calendar to determine how tasks will be scheduled. It is imperative that the calendar options match the project calendar to create a consistency in the scheduling values for tasks and assignment values.

To access the Calendar options:

Click **File → Options → Schedule**

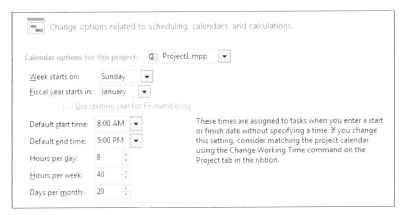

Figure 3-11   Calendar options should be adjusted if the calendar times are changed.

What the options mean:

- **Calendar options for this project**: option to select whether your choices for the calendar will be held within an individual project or if they will be applied to all new projects.
- **Week starts on**: this choice will affect what is assigned and viewed as the first day of the week. The day chosen will be reflected on the Gantt Chart, Resource Usage, Task Usage and other calendar views.
- **Fiscal Year starts in**: if using this option, select which month will be the start of the fiscal year.
- **Default start and end times**: these values should match the time values on the project calendar. Assigning the project calendar will

be discussed in the next lesson. The times stated here will be used to schedule tasks when time is not specified for a task. It will also be used to schedule tasks that do not use relationships. For example: if recurring tasks are created, the tasks will always be scheduled at the start time represented in this option.

- **Hours per day**: when 1 day of work is scheduled, how many hours should 1 day consist of?
- **Hours per week**: when 1 week of work is scheduled, how many hours should 1 week consist of?
- **Days per month**: when 1 month of work is scheduled, how many days should 1 month consist of?

Saving the Calendar

In Project 2013, the calendar that was just created is known as a "custom object". Custom objects may be saved for use in the project the object was created in and used in other projects as well. To save objects the Organizer is used. When Project 2013 was installed on your system, a file named Global.mpt was created. The Organizer is the function that will copy objects into the Global.mpt as well as between project schedules. Calendars are only one of many object types that may be customized and saved for use in other project schedules.

To save the customized calendar, the object must be copied using the Organizer.

To copy a New Base Calendar into the Global.mpt:

1. Click **File → Info → Organizer**
2. Click the **Calendars** tab
3. Click **Standard** to the right and click **<<Copy**
4. An error message will appear: "Do you want to replace the Standard in 'Global.mpt' with the Standard from '<project name.' Indicate "Yes."
5. Click **Cancel** to close the box

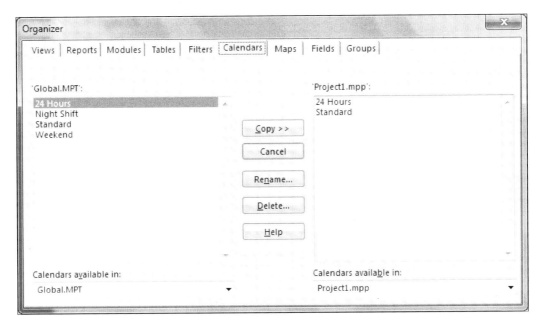

Figure 3-12   Use the Organizer to copy the updated calendar into your local Global.mpt file.

The Calendar will be copied into your local Global.mpt.

Project Information

The project information that should be entered before proceeding with project schedule development is the project start or project finish date as well as indicating which calendar will be used as the project calendar. This information is entered through the Project Information box.

To navigate to the Project Information dialog box:

Click **Project → Project Information**

Deciding whether to enter the Project Start date or the Project Finish date will take some consideration. There are pros and cons to either choice:

FAQ: Should I enter a project start and finish date?

Answer: Project 2013 will accept either the start or the finish date but not both.

Entering a start date will indicate that you are planning your schedule as forward scheduling. This will result in:

- All tasks will be scheduled As soon as possible
- The work of the project will determine the project ending date
- You will have a date to manage your project to, and know when you are on time or late with the progress of the project

Entering a finish date will indicate that you are planning your schedule as backward scheduling. This will result in:

- All tasks will be scheduled As late as possible
- The ending date of the project will be locked to a date on the calendar
- You might be planning a project where each task will be required to be completed as planned to achieve the ending date goals.

The most used planning method is that projects are planned from the project start date.

Project Calendar: The default calendar is "Standard". Whatever calendar is selected will become the scheduling calendar for the project. All tasks will be scheduled using this calendar until a resource is assigned to the task.

Click **OK** to close the box.

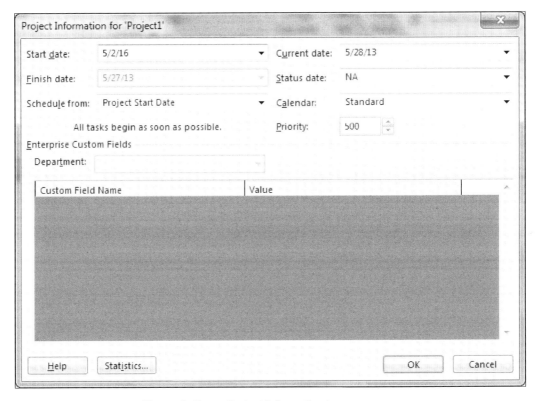

Figure 3-13   Project Information box.

Most project managers have definite deadlines. Consider planning the schedule from ending date to get the schedule short term goals, deadlines and milestone dates. Then switch the project to the start date to manage. Reset the constraints to as soon as possible to enable the schedule to include slack and aid in schedule management.

Options

The last action you should perform before entering your first task is to set some of the options to match the requirements of your project.

Options are flexible in that they can be applied per unique project or to all new projects created on your computer. In this section we will discuss the options that will affect scheduling. These options are in addition to the calendar options discussed earlier in this chapter.

General vs Per Project Options

General options are options which affect how the installation of Project 2013 on a desktop will operate. Per Project options are options that will apply to a unique project. You may optionally apply the per project options to all new projects.

Display options are options that will help the user interact with Project 2013 software. The options selected are unique to each user and are a personal preference. These options do not have an influence on the ability to create a project schedule.

To navigate to General options:

Click **File → Options → General**

In the Project view section, the user may select the default view for usage of Project 2013 and the date format for dates for reports and views (table portion of a view).

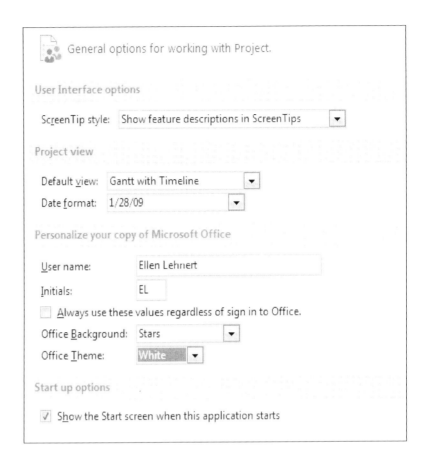

Figure 3-14   General Options view.

To navigate to Display options:

Click **File → Options → Display**

These options refer to which elements should be viewed on the screen. These options will control which indicators are shown in the indicator column, currency values and if the Entry bar is visible or not.

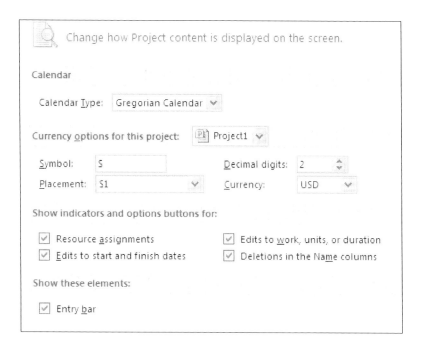

Figure 3-15   Display options view.

Additional display options are available at:

Click **File → Options → Advanced**

Some of the options that should be considered are:

- **Show this number of recent documents** – optional number, list will show in the Recent tab in the backstage
- **Automatically add new views, tables, filters and groups to the global** - recommended
- **Settings for duration label values** – Minutes, Days, etc. - may alter as needed
- **Show project summary task** – recommended

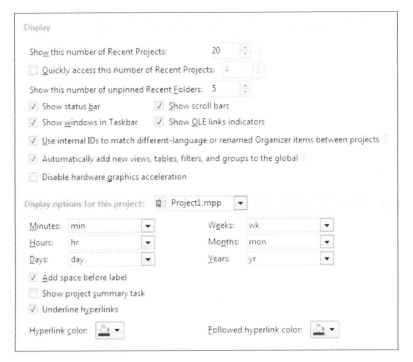

Figure 3-16   These display options are in the Advanced options section.

Each project schedule has the ability to contain a Project Summary task. The Project Summary task is a zero level task that will serve as a constant grand total for the project schedule. The setting in the above option may be used to turn on the project summary task by default for all projects.

To turn on the Project Summary task:

Click **Task → Gantt Chart**

Click **Format → Project Summary Task** (on the right side of the ribbon)

Scheduling Options

To understand the Scheduling options it would be helpful to review some of the scheduling terms the options are referring to.

Project's scheduling engine uses the terms "Duration" and "Work" which are fundamental to understanding project scheduling.

Definitions

- **Duration**:
  - Is a length of time i.e.: a day, a week, or a month
  - It is the amount of actual time that will pass before a task is completed
- **Work**:
  - Is the quantity of work that occurs i.e.: 8 hours in one day, 40 hours in a week
  - It is the amount of work (effort or man hours) which a resource(s) will work to complete the task

It is very helpful within an organization to have a standard for these terms (i.e., all work will be planned in hours and all durations will be planned in days).

Effort-driven scheduling

Tasks have the option of being scheduled using Effort-driven scheduling. Effort-driven scheduling is defined as when more workers are added to a task, the effort (or work) will be divided across the workers.

For example: A project has a task called "Moving Boxes". The work of the task is to move 100 boxes from location A to B. If one person moves the boxes, it will take 10 hours of duration moving 10 boxes per hour. However, if 2 people move the boxes it will take 5 hours, 3 people can accomplish this task in one-third of the original time, etc.

With effort-driven scheduling the duration of the task will shorten when more workers are added because the work is divided over the resources.

Understanding Task Types

Each task will be assigned a task type when the task is added to the schedule. Task types work hand-in-hand with the effort-driven option discussed above. Task types will determine how a task is scheduled and will have an effect on the assignment of the resources to the task. Task types are considered unique per task and may be set on a task by task basis.

The option setting is to establish the default task type you would like each task to acquire when it is entered. Task types may be changed to match the needs of the tasks at a later point in time.

Project 2013 allows for the following 3 task types:

- **Fixed Duration**: A fixed duration task is a task created with a fixed length of time. Fixed Duration tasks are also tied to dates.

Example: This training class. When the time scheduled for this class is over, the work of the class is completed.

- **Fixed Units**: Units means quantity of a resource. Fixed Units means that the resource assignment quantity is fixed for the task. Using this task type will result in the quantity of the units assigned to a task coupled with the availability of the resource to determine the scheduling of the task.

  Example: If you assign a resource to a 5 day, 40 hour task at 100% of their effort the task will be completed in 5 days working 8 hours per day. If you assign a resource to the same task with 50% of their effort, the task will be worked 4 hours per day and will be scheduled for 10 days of duration. The 100% and 50% are the resource units.

- **Fixed Work**: The work of the task is fixed. Fixed work tasks, by default, are also effort-driven. The more resources assigned to the task, the less time the task will take to be complete. Fixed work tasks will be scheduled based on the quantity of the units of the resources assigned to the task and their availability based on their resource calendar.

  Example: If a task called "Plan event" will take 80 hours of work to complete, the work will be completed in 2 weeks with 1 full time resource. If a second resource is added full time, the task will be completed in 1 week dividing the work between the 2 resources. Each resource would have performed 50% of the work. As resources are added to the task, the duration of the task is reduced.

Task type, Effort-driven combinations

When task types are coupled with the effort-driven option, the scheduling engine allows for the following task type, effort-driven combinations:

- Fixed Duration, Effort-driven on
- Fixed Duration, Effort-driven off
- Fixed Units, Effort-driven on
- Fixed Units, Effort-driven off
- Fixed Work, Effort-driven on

The project options will allow for setting a default that each task will be assigned when the task is entered. It should be noted that each task is different and unique. The default should be considered a starting point.

This is a brief introduction to this topic. Detailed coverage of task types and effort driven settings with assignments will be addressed throughout Chapter 8, *Work Assignments*.

Scheduling Options

Scheduling options are per project options which establish the defaults of how a project will be scheduled. These options are unique per project and should be checked before entering tasks into a project schedule. These options also may be changed at any time over the life of the project schedule.

To set the scheduling options:

Click **File → Options → Schedule**

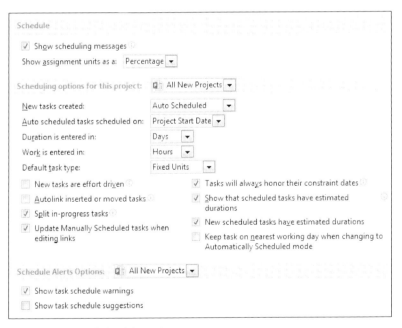

Figure 3-17   Schedule options.

- **Show scheduling messages**: gives the scheduler error messages concerning scheduling inconsistencies and warnings.
- **Show assignment units as a**: options are percentage or decimal. This is a user preference. It may be changed at any time without affecting the schedule.
- **Scheduling options for this project**: options that can be assigned to a specific project or all projects.
- **New tasks created**: manually scheduled or automatically scheduled. This is the default value and may be adjusted per task.
  - **Manually scheduled**: tasks will be entered without a start or finish date and without task duration. All values are entered manually.
  - **Auto scheduled**: tasks will be entered with a default duration of 1 day and a start and finish date.
- **Auto scheduled tasks scheduled on**: project state date or current date. If you are managing a long project it might be easier to change this option for all new tasks to start on the current date.
- **Duration is entered in**: minutes, hours, days, weeks, months
- **Work is entered in**: minutes, hours, days, weeks, months
- **Default task type**: Fixed Units, Fixed Duration, or Fixed Work
- **New tasks are effort driven**: check for yes
- **Update Manually Scheduled tasks when updating links**: when tasks are manually scheduled should the project schedule successor tasks adjust based on relationship links

It is a good idea within an organization to establish a standard for Duration and Work. When duration is discussed or appears on a report it will be easier for stakeholders to understand that duration always means hours or days or the value you choose as the standard for projects. If you have a 3 year project, you probably will not be planning work at the hour level so weeks might be the duration standard.

Key Points to Remember

- You can use a template or create a project from Excel or SharePoint tasks.
- Schedules can be saved into alternate formats including PDF, older versions of Project and Excel formats.
- The Project calendar is where corporate holidays are recorded. These holidays become non-working days in the schedule.
- Calendar options can be refined to tailor the Gantt Chart view or to better match the corporate working hours.
- Project information is where you set the scheduling mode and date the schedule calculates from.
- Within Project Options, general options apply to every schedule while per project options apply to only a specific schedule.
- Duration is the length of time for a task while Work is the hours for a task.
- Effort-driven scheduling means that work will be distributed across resources.
- A combination of task type and effort-driven settings may be used to achieve the desired task scheduling.

Chapter 4

Task Development

"The key is not to prioritize
what's on your schedule, but
to schedule your priorities."

~ Stephen Covey

Overview

In planning out a schedule, you will need to consider which life cycle approach you will be applying. Three popular options are Work Breakdown Structure (WBS), Agile, and Waterfall. Each approach has benefits and will support various business scenarios. After the life cycle is decided, it will be important to build a task list using an organized hierarchy of tasks which can be expanded or collapsed to illustrate various phases of a project. In addition to a hierarchy, a project will include milestones or check points. Schedules can include automatic or manually scheduled tasks to support the preferred life cycle approach.

Project Life Cycle Approach to Scheduling

There are many different planning or scheduling methodologies for project management. In the 20+ years of using technologies that support scheduling, planning and resource demand and capacity planning, we the authors have experienced and heard that Project is not a good tool for certain types of lifecycle planning.

This is clearly untrue. If you think about what scheduling technologies are, they are simply relational databases. It is the approach of how you setup, layout or build a schedule or project plan that makes it better or worse.

Yes some tools have pre-built views, reports or tend to be used in certain industries (like construction), but that has been a product of the history of these technologies and the need for that type of tool. For example it really has only been in the last 20 years that IT, system, and software development has really exploded. In comparison engineering or construction projects have been ongoing for centuries.

What we hope you learn from this section is that it is up to you and how you would like to organize, view, track, report and manage a schedule that determines its ability to support you in the Project Lifecycle that you are using.

Remember Microsoft Project is a relational database, just like almost every other scheduling tools (some are just flat files, like Excel), but for our discussion today, we are only considering true scheduling technologies.

Where Microsoft Project has grown and overshadowed every other scheduling tool out there by volume of purchases, is the simplicity, flexibility and ease of use that the tool provides to its user.

With a little thought you can make Project behave and support any lifecycle methodology approach to scheduling. Whether Scrum, SDLC, Lean, Waterfall, etc. you have the same functional components for managing a project. Namely the following:

- Fields (native and custom)
- Sorting Capabilities
- Grouping
- Filtering
- Views & Reports

Remember, demand, work, deliverables, tasks, activities are all the same object. A task is a row that has data and meta-data associated to it. That means you can have a column for your task that identifies its properties. For example a task about "rollout training for end users" can be organized by phase, type of work (training), by department, who will deliver it, even by the skillset needed.

As you will see in the next few sections, you can take that activity or task and organize it any way you like, it still represents demand, work or something that has a typical time-phased activity that needs to be scheduled.

We hope you open your mind and think about using Project in many different lifecycle planning and managing approaches and find the combination that works best for you and the projects that you are managing.

WBS Scheduling Approach

The concept behind Work Breakdown Structure (WBS) scheduling is to arrange work packages or work elements (tasks) into a grouping of activities that have a common element to them. For example, documentation tasks may occur across the entire project, but are grouped, estimated and planned and in many cases invoiced in common location within the schedule.

Work Breakdown Structure (WBS) is a tool / methodology that defines a project grouping of a project's discrete work elements (tasks) in a way that helps organize and define the total work scope of the project.

A project manager must have both a WBS and related estimates to define a project schedule (a project schedule is the series of activities that link the tasks to be done with the resources that will do the work). The project schedule is part of the project plan (not the whole plan, but an artifact of the project plan).

A great value that a WBS creates is it allows you to organize and decompose a larger set of tasks into a smaller subset of related activities. Remember that this is an exercise that isn't about sequencing, but more focused on establishing tasks and estimates.

The advantage of using a WBS is that you can quickly get to a proper level of detail. The proper level will be dependent upon the needs / culture of the Project Manager, the Organization or the work being planned.

A common misunderstanding is that a project schedule has to stay lined out or organized in this manner. While it may be easier to see organized types of work, it becomes more difficult to manage the related work activities.

Remember that Project is a relational database and we can group tasks quickly and efficiently based upon simple common fields or values within the project tasks (i.e. a custom column).

Key Benefits of WBS Scheduling

- Organizing Key Activities, Deliverables by Functionality or Activity Type
- Excellent approach to working with a team to map out key work activities
- Break out larger work deliverables into manageable and assignable work
- Easy to see all like work grouped or in a localized area
- Fast references to work that can be collapsed by section
- Typically aligned with a BOM or SOW/Contract deliverables for billing

In Project, you may require that your WBS be related to Accounting or Other Tracking Systems. If your project would benefit from having detailed

WBS codes that are made up of specific lengths, sequences, or sets of numbers and letters, you can define a custom WBS code mask (a code mask is the character format that you define for a custom field). The custom WBS code is recorded in the WBS field.

As with outline numbers, each level of a custom WBS code represents an outline level (outline level: The number of levels that a task is indented from the top level of the outline. You can in-dent tasks up to 65,000 levels in Project.) in the task list. You can use a unique format for each level of the code, and each level is listed in the code according to the hierarchy of tasks, summary tasks, and subtasks.

So clearly you have room to grow, organize your project schedule.

Figure 4-1 is an example of a Project Schedule Organized in a Work Breakdown Structure format. The overall concept is that WBS is about work activities.

Resource Name	Work	Details	11	18	25	1	8	15
⊟ **Name: Amy McKay**	128 h	Work	16h	24h	16h	36h	8h	28h
⊟ 3 Renovation	128 h	Work						
⊟ 3.1 Construction	128 h	Work						
⊟ 3.1.1 Carpentry	128 h	Work	16h	24h	16h	36h	8h	28h
Strip walls	*16 h*	Work	16h					
Remove asbestos in ceiling	*40 h*	Work		24h	16h			
Asbestos removal inspection	*4 h*	Work				4h		
Frame new walls	*16 h*	Work				16h		
Put up dry wall	*16 h*	Work				16h		
Plaster	*8 h*	Work					8h	
Install new cabinets	*4 h*	Work						4h
Paint cabinets	*4 h*	Work						4h
Lay new flooring	*8 h*	Work						8h
Install appliances	*8 h*	Work						8h
Carpentry Inspection	*4 h*	Work						4h
⊟ **Name: Bob Siclari**	56 h	Work					40h	16h
⊟ 3 Renovation	56 h	Work						
⊟ 3.1 Construction	56 h	Work						
⊟ 3.1.5 Plumbing	56 h	Work					40h	16h
Install pipes	*40 h*	Work					40h	

Figure 4-1   WBS Methodology Scheduling Approach.

We encourage you to try using a WBS to help map out key deliverables and activities. What is wonderful about Project 2013 is that there are a myriad of different tools you can plan and organize your project in and then simply by using the Rich Copy/Paste features and the manual scheduling, to drop that in and begin the estimating, linking and establishing a dynamic schedule. By leveraging the simplistic approach of a WBS, you can rapidly build a schedule, feel confident that you have not missed key planning tasks and activities and then sequence the work, thereby establishing relationships between your dependent tasks.

Agile Methodology Scheduling Approach

As mentioned above, Agile, Scrum or other Agile approaches to project scheduling take on a more iterative approach and feel.

A common misconception is that Project cannot handle this or isn't designed for this. This is clearly not the case. Remember Project is a database and can be laid out to sort, group, filter, and organize work into views based upon data at the task level.

In today's ever growing IT and software development world, the work is in many times iterative, however that is not limited to just IT work. In engineering projects, in many cases there are a series of design / build (30%, 60% and 90%) cycles of work that touch or retouch pieces of project work.

What is nice about using iterative planning and scheduling approaches (Agile) is that you can break apart the work by features and activities relating the activities to those feature sets that need completed.

Key Benefits of Agile Scheduling

- Highly Iterative and easily to clone sections that dynamically build off of each other.
- Burn Down Charts, Views, Sprints and Groupings allow for Easy to follow Work Deliverables.
- Manual Scheduling and Integration with other Scheduling Tools (Team Foundation Server).
- Provides a way for work to be broken up into iterative (Sprints) and aligned with key categories or summary activities, such as a Software Development Lifecycle (SDLC).

In *Figure 4-2*, we illustrate lining out the key features (un-named), but essentially the tasks that need to be managed based upon the Sprint, priority, customer need, etc.

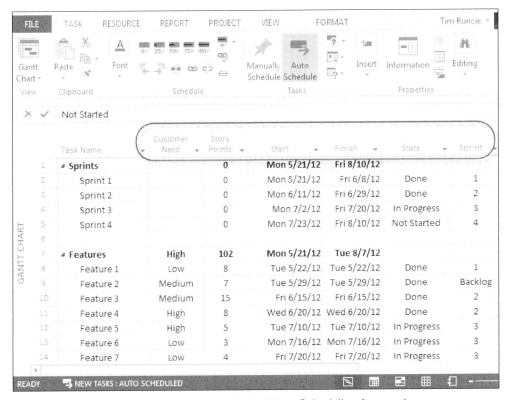

Figure 4-2   Agile Methodology Scheduling Approach.

In *Figure 4-3*, we use the project's fields to group by a Burn Down view, showcasing features, sprints and key work that is being managed, by simply grouping by the state of the work (done, in progress, backlog, etc.).

Remember you can quickly and efficiently embed these as tables or views in project to quickly re-organize the schedule back into any manner of layout (WBS, Waterfall, etc.) as desired.

	Task Name	Customer Need	Story Points	Start	Finish	State	Sprint
	◢ **Done**		**47**	**Mon 5/21/12**	**Fri 6/29/12**		
	▷ 1		**11**	**Mon 5/21/12**	**Fri 6/8/12**		
	◢ 2		**29**	**Mon 6/11/12**	**Fri 6/29/12**		
3	Sprint 2		0	Mon 6/11/12	Fri 6/29/12	Done	2
10	Feature 3	Medium	15	Fri 6/15/12	Fri 6/15/12	Done	2
11	Feature 4	High	8	Wed 6/20/12	Wed 6/20/12	Done	2
22	Feature 15	Low	6	Fri 6/29/12	Fri 6/29/12	Done	2
	◢ **Backlog**		**7**	**Tue 5/29/12**	**Tue 5/29/12**		
9	Feature 2	Medium	7	Tue 5/29/12	Tue 5/29/12	Done	Backlog
	◢ **In Progress**		**17**	**Mon 7/2/12**	**Tue 8/7/12**		
	◢ 3		**12**	**Mon 7/2/12**	**Fri 7/20/12**		
4	Sprint 3		0	Mon 7/2/12	Fri 7/20/12	In Progress	3
12	Feature 5	High	5	Tue 7/10/12	Tue 7/10/12	In Progress	3
13	Feature 6	Low	3	Mon 7/16/12	Mon 7/16/12	In Progress	3
14	Feature 7	Low	4	Fri 7/20/12	Fri 7/20/12	In Progress	3
	◢ 4		**5**	**Tue 8/7/12**	**Tue 8/7/12**		
15	Feature 8	Low	5	Tue 8/7/12	Tue 8/7/12	In Progress	4
	◢ **Not Started**		**38**	**Mon 5/21/12**	**Fri 8/10/12**		

Figure 4-3   Agile Methodology Grouping

Waterfall (Project Lifecycle by Phase) Scheduling Approach

While we can write an entire book on just the Waterfall approach to planning and scheduling, we want to introduce the idea of waterfall planning activities that follow a lifecycle: phases, stages and timelapsed series of work activities.

This is very common in planning. Do note that in some portions of a project schedule, there are iterative or agile activities. These can be embedded and managed within on overall waterfall project schedule.

Waterfall scheduling methodology is very popular for the systems development lifecycle model for software development. The waterfall model defines a development method that is linear and sequential, with tasks following each other leading to a deliverable or a milestone for each phase of development. The overall concept that time phased work flows forward. Once a phase of development is completed, the development proceeds to the next phase and it is not revisited.

The advantage of waterfall development is that it allows for work to be segmented and managed by functional groups or departments. A schedule can be set with deadlines for each stage of development and a product can proceed through the development process similar to an assembly line, and theoretically, be delivered on time. Development moves through phases, typically from concept, through design, implementation, testing, installation, troubleshooting, and ends up at operation and maintenance. In most waterfall planning, the phases of development proceed in strict order, without any overlapping or iterative steps.

The disadvantage of waterfall development is that it does not allow for much reflection or revision and if there are iterations that need to revisit or retouch work, the planning layout has to be handled differently. A good example is that once an application is in testing, it is very difficult to go back and change something that was not well-thought out in the concept stage. Other approaches or supplemental approaches to the waterfall methodology include joint application development (JAD), rapid application development (RAD), or sometimes Joint Rapid Application Development (JRAD), to update, fix and address product or solution defects.

Key Benefits of Waterfall Scheduling

- Easy to Organize and Visualize planning and managing of project work activities
- It can and is used for System or Software Development
- Works well for assigning large work to different groups to manage and hand off
- Lays out timeline planning for deliverable driven planning
- Project goes through a distinct lifecycle, from requirements to design, implementation, testing and deployment

Figure 4-4 is an example of Waterfall scheduling, also organized by a phased lifecycle. Remember that Waterfall organizes tasks that traditionally have a path or predecessor / successor relationship and unfold linearly.

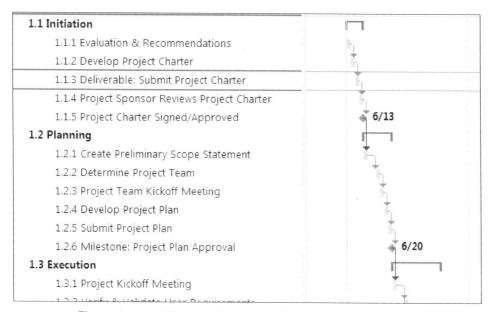

Figure 4-4   Waterfall Methodology Scheduling Approach.

Creating the Work Breakdown Structure

Once the tasks of the project are established, the next step is to enter the tasks into the project schedule and create a WBS structure. Entering tasks may be a manual keying process or they may be imported from a SharePoint list (Project 2013 Pro only), an Excel workbook, an Outlook task list or a Word document. Tasks may also be copy and pasted into project schedules. This lesson addresses the manual entering of tasks into the project schedule.

In this lesson, we will discuss:

- WBS
- Entering tasks
- The Task Information Form
- Outlining tasks into a WBS Hierarchy
- Displaying WBS code values
- Customizing WBS code numbers
- Manual vs Automatic

Overview of Work Breakdown Structure

The next step in creating a project schedule is to enter the tasks for the project. What work should be planned and how should the tasks be organized? The Work Breakdown Structure or WBS is the task list for the project. How the WBS is structured will influence reports that are generated from the schedule and ease of managing the schedule. These questions and others need to be answered in order to create a project schedule that will help you manage your projects.

What is a Work Breakdown Structure or WBS?

Simple projects like packing for a trip might not need a plan to accomplish the project. When packing, most people will make of list of the items to pack. Everything on the list is added to the suitcase and the project is completed. Not all projects are this simple.

Larger projects like building a house will require more planning and detail to accomplish the goals of the project. More data and tasks will be created depending on how the project is to be performed. To accomplish these types of projects, a work breakdown structure or WBS will be required.

The WBS is a hierarchical structure much like an outline list. This structure will contain the work of the project. When developing a WBS the total work of the project is divided into chucks of work. The larger chucks are subdivided into smaller chucks. After the work is divided it is then organized into a hierarchical structure. Within the structure some tasks will serve as titles, some tasks will be goal points and others will contain task work details.

Consider the WBS of a project the same as the foundation for a building. Without a solid foundation the building will not be stable. Having a stable or well-planned WBS will be an asset to the performance of a project. Having an unstable WBS may adversely affect the management of the project schedule.

Task Categories

When building a WBS using MS Project 2013 there are 4 categories of tasks available to use. The categories are:

Project Summary Task: This is a task that will provide a title and a grand total for the project. It is the top level task (level 0) and it can be turned on and off as needed.

Summary Tasks: These tasks are section titles that will also provide subtotals throughout the project.

Tasks or Detail Tasks: These are work tasks within the project. Work tasks will carry the work and duration for the project as well as costs. Resources or workers will be assigned here and tracking will occur for these tasks.

Milestones: Milestones are points in time. They become the goal points within the project and can provide high level timeline reports.

Entering Tasks

Entering tasks into Project 2013 is as easy as typing the task name into the Task Name field. When entering a new task, keep in mind that data is being populated in an array of fields for that row; several hundred fields will be created and some populated. After tasks are entered they may be moved, deleted, or copy/pasted to other areas of the schedule. It is also recommended that the Project Summary Task be turned on to aid in schedule development.

To turn on the Project Summary task:

- Click on **Format → Project Summary Task** (In the show/hide section on the right)
- Click the **check box** to turn on

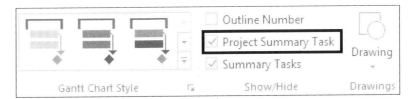

Figure 4-5   Project Summary Task.

To enter a new task:

- Click the **Task Name** field on the row you would like to enter and type the task name.

To move a task to another location in the schedule:

- Left Click on the task number (ID) in the left column. Position the mouse pointer on the task number and wait for the 4 way arrow to appear and drag the task to the new location. (Works well when the new location can be seen on the screen)
    OR
- Click on the **task number** of the task you wish to move
- Click **cut**
- Scroll to the new location
- Click **Paste** – Project 2013 will insert the pasted task

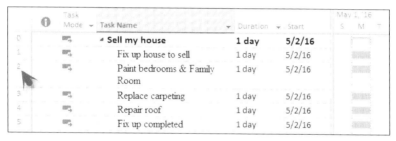

Figure 4-6   Task number.

Entering blank lines to receive the moved tasks is not necessary. The schedule will insert the lines and move tasks down to accommodate the moved tasks.

To add blank lines in the schedule between existing tasks:

- Right click on the **task** below the location of the new task to be inserted
- Click **Task → Task** (Insert group) – a blank row will be created above the task selected
    OR
- Click on a task
- Click **Insert** key on the keyboard

In the view below task 6 was entered using the Task → Task insert method. Note the default data and <New Task> name entered. Task 8 was the result of clicking the Insert key on the keyboard.

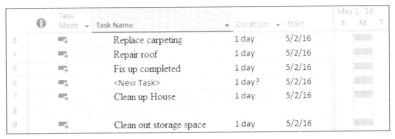

	①	Task Mode ▾	Task Name ▾	Duration ▾	Start	May 1, '16 S	M	T
3		⊟,	Replace carpeting	1 day	5/2/16			
4		⊟,	Repair roof	1 day	5/2/16			
5		⊟,	Fix up completed	1 day	5/2/16			
6		⊟,	<New Task>	1 day?	5/2/16			
7		⊟,	Clean up House	1 day	5/2/16			
8								
9		⊟,	Clean out storage space	1 day	5/2/16			

Figure 4-7   Task 6 was created by clicking on the "Clean Up House" task and click on the Insert → Task button on the Task ribbon. Task 8 was created by clicking on the "Clean out storage space" task clicking the Insert key on the keyboard.

To delete tasks from the schedule:

- Right click the task number to be deleted
- Click **Delete Task** option
  OR
- Click the task number to be deleted
- Click the Delete key on the keyboard

> If you have clicked anywhere within the task row and attempted to delete the task a Smart Tag will appear to ask if you want to clear the field or delete the task row.

In the view below the result of clicking on the Smart Tag (the X with the down arrow) is shown. Make your selection from the choices in the box below.

3		Replace carpeting	1 day	5/2/16	
4		Repair roof	1 day	5/2/16	
5		Fix up completed	1 day	5/2/16	
6		<New Task>	1 day?	5/2/16	
7		Clean up House	1 day	5/2/16	
8	X ▾		1 day	5/2/16	
9	⊕	Delete the task name.	1 day	5/2/16	
10	○	Delete the task.	1 day	5/2/16	
11		Clean up completed	1 day	5/2/16	

Figure 4-8   Smart tag asking the user to select if the task name should be cleared or the entire task deleted.

Moving and Copying Tasks

If you want to create a task that is similar to an existing task, you can copy the existing task and then modify the copy.

To copy a task:

1. Select the entire row of the task you want to copy by clicking on its ID field. If you only want to copy one field, such as the task name, select only that field.
2. In the **Task** Tab, **Clipboard** group, click **Copy**. Project copies the task to the Clipboard.
3. Select the task below the line the task will be inserted.
4. In the **Task** tab, **Clipboard** group, click **Paste**.

> Keyboard shortcuts Ctrl+C (copy) and Ctrl+V (paste) will work as well.

You can also copy a single cell of data, rather than the entire task row.

> Be aware that when you paste the contents of a single field, Project overwrites the contents of the field into which you paste. If you paste the single field into a blank row, Project creates a new task.

To move a task:

1. Click the ID number of the task to select the entire row.
2. Drag the entire task to the new location, between two existing tasks.

> If you drag the contents of a single field to another field, Project overwrites the contents of the field.

If you move a task that is within a series of tasks that are linked sequentially, Project automatically adjusts the link relationships of the remaining tasks to reflect the new task order. Project does this only if the current task is linked to the task directly above and below. The moved task will maintain the original link to predecessors. Linking to a new series will need to be done manually.

Task Information Form

The Task Information box is a source of easy access for some of the frequently used fields on the task side of the data for a Project 2013 project schedule. Data entered in the form is the same as entering data into a column in a table for a task. Using this box is a quick and easy way to view and maintain task information.

To access the Task Information Form:

- Double click an **task data** field within a task
  - OR
- Click on a **task**
- **Task** tab → **Information**

The dialog box below will appear:

Figure 4-9   Task info box.

The dialog contains several tabs of information, grouped by subject. Each tab will allow access to the Task name, Duration and Estimated flag.

General tab: contains Name, Duration, Percent complete, Priority, Schedule Mode, Inactive, Start and Finish dates, Display on Timeline, Hide Bar and Rollup.

Predecessors: contains information concerning task relationships.

Resources: contains information concerning resources assigned to the task.

Advanced: contains information concerning Deadlines, Constraints, Task Types, Task Calendars, Effort-driven flag, WBS number and Milestone flag for the task.

Notes: general notes area for the task

Custom fields: If task level custom fields (user-defined) were created for the project, they would be accumulated and accessible through this area.

Data may be changed in multiple tasks at the same time. Select the tasks to be changed and then click on the Information icon on the Task tab. The dialog that appears is called Multiple Task Information. Make the changes and click **OK** to update.

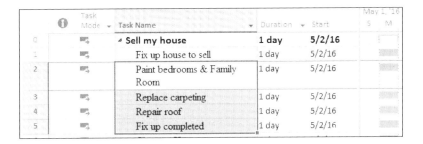

Figure 4-10   Select multiple tasks.

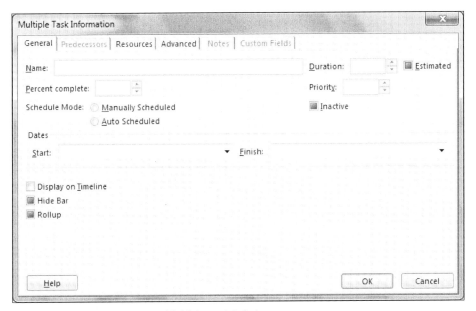

Figure 4-11   Multiple task info box.

Outlining Tasks into a Hierarchy

Once tasks are entered, the WBS outline structure may be created. To create the outline structure, tasks will be indented or outdented. These buttons are located on the Task tab in the Schedule group and are the green arrows in the lower left corner. The indent button is pointing to the right. The outdent button is pointing to the left. See below:

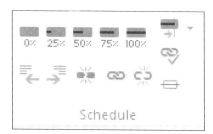

Figure 4-12   Schedule section of Task ribbon bar. Outdent is in the lower left corner, arrow pointing to the left. Indent has the Arrow pointing to the right.

To indent a task:

- Click the task to be indented
- Click the **indent** (pointing right green arrow)
    OR
- Place the mouse pointer over the task and a horizontal arrow will appear. Left click and drag the task to the right

To outdent a task or remove an indention:

- Click the task to be outdented
- Click the **outdent** (left pointing green arrow)
    OR
- Place the mouse pointer over the task and a horizontal arrow will appear. Left click and drag the task to the left

When a task has an indented task below it, the task becomes a summary task. Summary tasks are represented as black bars on the Gantt chart as shown below:

Task Name	Duration	Start	May 1, '16 S	M
◢ **Sell my house**	**1 day**	**5/2/16**		
◢ **Fix up house to sell**	**1 day**	**5/2/16**		
Paint bedrooms & Family Room	1 day	5/2/16		
Replace carpeting	1 day	5/2/16		
Repair roof	1 day	5/2/16		
Fix up completed	1 day	5/2/16		

Figure 4-13   The task named "Fix up house to sell" became a Summary task when all of the tasks below it were indented. Note the summary task formatting on the Gantt Chart.

Indenting and outdenting can be confusing. At times it is difficult to achieve the desired structure results.

When indenting, work from the top down. When outdenting, work from the bottom up.

To see the levels of the WBS:

Project Summary tasks and Summary Tasks will have a small box to the left of the summary task name as seen in the screen above.

- Click the **plus** sign + to expand tasks
- Click the **minus** sign – to collapse tasks

Use the Outline button to jump to a level of detail:

Click on **View → Outline**:

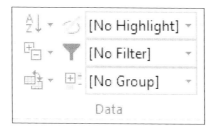

Figure 4-14   The Outline button is in the Data section of the View ribbon bar. Use this button to view various levels of the WBS.

When the **Outline** down arrow is clicked, the following choices appear:

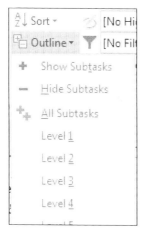

Figure 4-15   Clicking on the Outline button will reveal choices for selecting the outline detail level to view.

The following image shows a view of a collapsed WBS – **Outline level 1** was selected. Note the rolled up view of the tasks:

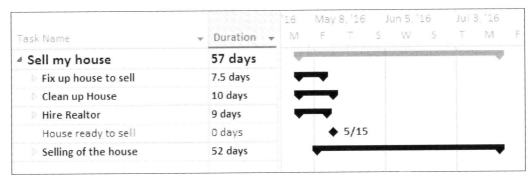

Task Name	Duration
⊿ **Sell my house**	**57 days**
▷ Fix up house to sell	7.5 days
▷ Clean up House	10 days
▷ Hire Realtor	9 days
House ready to sell	0 days
▷ Selling of the house	52 days

Figure 4-16   The result of selecting Outline 1 which will collapse the detail to the highest level.

The following image shows a view of an expanded outline WBS – **All Subtasks** was selected:

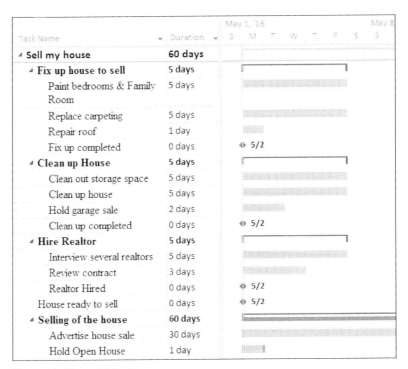

Task Name	Duration
⊿ **Sell my house**	**60 days**
⊿ **Fix up house to sell**	**5 days**
Paint bedrooms & Family Room	5 days
Replace carpeting	5 days
Repair roof	1 day
Fix up completed	0 days
⊿ **Clean up House**	**5 days**
Clean out storage space	5 days
Clean up house	5 days
Hold garage sale	2 days
Clean up completed	0 days
⊿ **Hire Realtor**	**5 days**
Interview several realtors	5 days
Review contract	3 days
Realtor Hired	0 days
House ready to sell	0 days
⊿ **Selling of the house**	**60 days**
Advertise house sale	30 days
Hold Open House	1 day

Figure 4-17   All tasks.

Clicking **Project Summary** task and then **Hide Subtasks** will collapse the project down to just the Project Summary task.

If the outline is collapsed, clicking **All Subtasks** will show all tasks at all levels of the WBS.

The outline list offers the option to create up to 9 WBS levels. There are many more levels available in Project 2013 but it is advised that WBS levels should not exceed 5. The more WBS levels there are, the more confusing and cumbersome a WBS may become.

Displaying Outline Numbers & WBS

As the WBS structure is created, an automatic numbering sequence is also created within the task list. The numbers represent where in the WBS structure the tasks reside. This is a unique numbering scheme and numbers are automatically reassigned as tasks are moved around the WBS structure. There are default number values and customized WBS number values. In this lesson, we will address the standard WBS values; the following lesson will address the customized values available.

To insert the WBS column into a table:

- To insert a column into a table, right click on the column header to the right of where you would like the inserted column to be located.
- Select Insert Column
- Click the W key on the keyboard
- Select "WBS"
- Click OK

> After the column is inserted it may be moved to an alternate location if needed.

Refer to *Figure 4-18*, an example of a WBS numbering schema:

WBS	Task Name
0	⊿ **Sell my house**
1	⊿ **Fix up house to sell**
1.1	Paint bedrooms & Family Room
1.2	Replace carpeting
1.3	Repair roof
1.4	Fix up completed
2	⊿ **Clean up House**
2.1	Clean out storage space
2.2	Clean up house
2.3	Hold garage sale
2.4	Clean up completed
3	⊿ **Hire Realtor**
3.1	Interview several realtors
3.2	Review contract
3.3	Realtor Hired
4	House ready to sell
5	⊿ **Selling of the house**
5.1	Advertise house sale
5.2	Hold Open House
5.3	House on the market
5.4	Review contracts
5.5	House Sold

Figure 4-18   The WBS column is displaying the system assigned WBS numbers associated with the tasks.

Because automatic WBS numbers are updated as tasks are moved or added to the WBS, it is not recommended that these numbers be used as a task tracking number. If a task tracking number is desired, consider using the field called "Unique ID". This field is the order, in which tasks were added to the schedule and they will always be unique and will not be duplicated within a schedule.

Collapsing and Expanding the Outline

One of the main benefits of outlining is that you can control the level of detail that Project displays. For example, if you want to inform upper management about the status of your project, they may not be interested in the daily tasks, only the major phases. You have the option to collapse the outline to display only summary tasks, you can expand the outline to display all of the tasks, or you can display the subtasks for some summary tasks, but not for others.

There are carat symbols to the left of the Summary task names. Clicking on these symbols will allow for expanding or collapsing of the WBS. If the carat is black and pointing down (◢), that means all of the tasks are expanded for that summary grouping. If the carat is clear and pointing to the right (▷), the summary grouping is collapsed.

To collapse the schedule outline:

1. Select the desired Summary task.
2. Click the ◢ to the left of the Summary task.

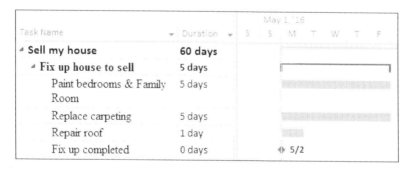

Figure 4-19   Expanded task details.

To expand the schedule outline:

1. Select the desired Summary task.
2. Click the ◢ to the left of the Summary task.

Clean up House	5 days	
Hire Realtor	5 days	

Figure 4-20   Collapsed task detail.

Customizing WBS Codes

The user has the option of customizing WBS numbers using a custom code with settings entered by the user. When this option is evoked, additional options to re-number the WBS, enforce value uniqueness and optionally generate WBS numbers becomes available. The customized number values are helpful when managing multiple projects or if there is a need to reference numbers unique to a project schedule. They are also helpful if using templates that result in frequently used task names. These codes could indicate which tasks are members of which project schedules and where the tasks are located within the project schedule.

To customize the WBS numbers:

- Project → WBS button → Define

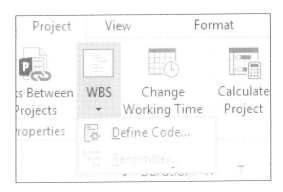

Figure 4-21   WBS define code box.

- **Project Code Prefix**: use this value to enter a code that will represent an abbreviation that applies to all WBS numbers for the project schedule.

- **Sequence**: select the data type for the Code Mask to be created (i.e., Numbers, Uppercase Letters, Lower case Letters or Characters)
- **Length**: number of characters allowed
- **Separator**: symbol - . , - + or /

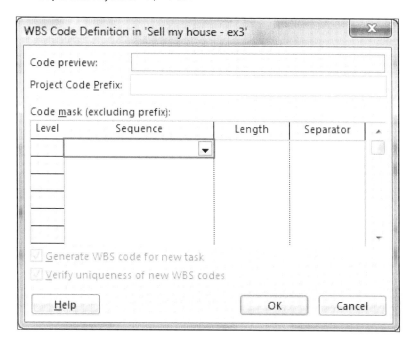

Figure 4-22   Use the above form when defining a customized WBS code for your project schedule.

Select as many lines as necessary to create your outline levels and click **OK**

Figure 4-23 is an example of a customized WBS code:

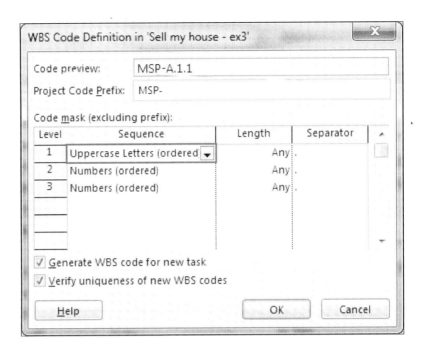

Figure 4-23   Example of customized WBS code mask.

Figure 4-24 is the result of the customized WBS values:

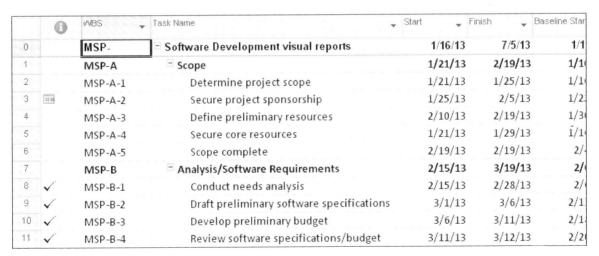

		WBS	Task Name	Start	Finish	Baseline Star
0		MSP-	⊟ **Software Development visual reports**	**1/16/13**	**7/5/13**	**1/1**
1		**MSP-A**	⊟ Scope	**1/21/13**	**2/19/13**	**1/1**
2		MSP-A-1	Determine project scope	1/21/13	1/25/13	1/1
3	▦	MSP-A-2	Secure project sponsorship	1/25/13	2/5/13	1/2
4		MSP-A-3	Define preliminary resources	2/10/13	2/19/13	1/3
5		MSP-A-4	Secure core resources	1/21/13	1/29/13	1/1
6		MSP-A-5	Scope complete	2/19/13	2/19/13	2/
7		**MSP-B**	⊟ **Analysis/Software Requirements**	**2/15/13**	**3/19/13**	**2/**
8	✓	MSP-B-1	Conduct needs analysis	2/15/13	2/28/13	2/
9	✓	MSP-B-2	Draft preliminary software specifications	3/1/13	3/6/13	2/1
10	✓	MSP-B-3	Develop preliminary budget	3/6/13	3/11/13	2/1
11	✓	MSP-B-4	Review software specifications/budget	3/11/13	3/12/13	2/2

Figure 4-24   Display of view containing customized WBS values.

When a WBS code is created, the options to **Generate a new WBS** for a new task and **Verify uniqueness of new WBS codes** become available.

To renumber the tasks based on the code values:

- **Project → WBS → Renumber**

Renumbering may be applied to selected tasks only or the entire project.

Be aware:

To remove a level: delete lower level row entries first and work upwards to higher levels.

After removing the level, the WBS number will not revert back to an unformatted state but will retain the previously applied code.

If WBS values are turned on as part of the task name the original non-formatted value appears and not the customized value. To turn on the WBS value as part of the task name:

From the Gantt Chart click: **View → Outline number**

The WBS numbers are shown below included with the task names:

WBS	Task Name	Duration
MSP-	⊿ **Sell my house**	**60 days**
MSP-A	⊿ **1 Fix up house to sell**	**5 days**
MSP-A.1	1.1 Paint bedrooms & Family Room	5 days
MSP-A.2	1.2 Replace carpeting	5 days
MSP-A.3	1.3 Repair roof	1 day
MSP-A.4	1.4 Fix up completed	0 days
MSP-B	⊿ **2 Clean up House**	**5 days**
MSP-B.1	2.1 Clean out storage space	5 days
MSP-B.2	2.2 Clean up house	5 days

Figure 4-25   WBS numbers included as part of the task name.

Guidelines for Creating a WBS

By following some guidelines for creating your Work Breakdown Structure, you can achieve a more effective and manageable project schedule. The WBS's purpose is to help manage a project schedule. When created without guidelines, the project schedule is in danger of becoming another project.

- The WBS is not a to-do list. Are you managing tasks or are you managing a to–do checklist? Usually, tasks or deliverables are entered into the project schedule. Checklists or Work Breakdown Structure dictionaries which contain more detail of how to accomplish the tasks are kept in another location such as a Word Document, Excel Workbook or SharePoint list.
- Identify deliverables within the WBS. Work from deliverable to deliverable in the development of the schedule.
- Break the deliverables into assignable work. When the task is at too high a level, establishing the work, assignments, order and relationships between tasks becomes more difficult.

- Establish a standard design for each section of work. An example of this would be:

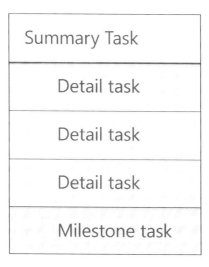

Summary Task
Detail task
Detail task
Detail task
Milestone task

Figure 4-26   Standard design example.

Using this format will allow for creating high level reports (Milestone reports) easily as well as moving sections of deliverables around easily.

- A naming standard for tasks is helpful and establishes consistency:
  - **Summary tasks**: these names should be nouns that describe the work to be completed in the section of work.

    Examples: Location, Network design, Clean-up, Foundations, Development, Requirements. Training, Pilot, Unit Testing
  - **Detail tasks**: should be action verbs and a noun which describes the work that is to be completed for the task.

    Examples: Build test database, Review requirements, Develop preliminary budget, Create training materials, Modify code
  - **Milestones**: should be used as goal dates within a project schedule. Naming standards for milestones should be past-tense adverbs.

    Examples: Development completed, Vendors contracted, New Facility Opened, Software selected, Integration testing completed
- Every summary task should have at least two subtasks. Detail tasks and milestones can be in the WBS without being part of a summary task grouping.

- Establish maximum and minimum lengths of duration for tasks. Create a rule of thumb based on the length of each project. For example: If you have a 6 month project no task should be less than 1 day and no task will be longer than 2 weeks. Use the rule as a guide for estimating task lengths. If tasks are too long, break the work down further.
- Decide if you will be creating a WBS in the rolling wave approach. The rolling wave approach is used for schedules managing software development or any schedule where all of the details of the project are not known at the beginning of the project. Consider creating placeholders for future phases of the project and elaborate the work one phase at a time.
- Deliverables: Completing a section of work means that the deliverable of that section has been accepted. Create a task for the delivery of the deliverable and create a milestone to represent the acceptance of the deliverable. The two rarely occur at the same time.
- Level of detail. The WBS may contain as many levels of detail as you need but best practices suggest that the more levels the more complex the schedule becomes. Recommendations suggest that the detail is manageable using five or less levels.
- If too much detail is put into the project schedule, the schedule will become a project unto itself. The more tasks, the more work.
- Use the WBS to help manage the scope of your project. If the task isn't in the project, consider it out of scope. When you enter tasks into the project schedule, ask yourself if the task is necessary.
- When planning the WBS think about just the work of the project. Many project managers like to start thinking about who will do the work and when. It is a good idea to focus on the work of the project only and think of the work as the "what" of the project. The "who" and "when" will come as the project schedule develops.
- Having the project team or the top level resources help build the WBS for a project is a win-win for the project:
  - Increases resource buy in
  - Encourages resource contribution
  - Provides feedback on problems from different angles
  - Lowers probability of missing tasks
  - Encourages team building

Milestones

A milestone is a check point in your project. It is a status, not a task which means that it has no duration and no resources are needed. For example, an approval or sign-off before the project can proceed and the completion of a stage of the project are both milestones. To Project, a milestone is a task with a zero duration.

To enter a milestone, use the following steps:

3. Insert a new task, or click the Task Name of a blank task.
4. Type the name for the milestone in the **Task Name** field and press the **Tab** key.
5. Type "0" in the Duration field, and press the Enter key.

Milestones are denoted in the Gantt Chart as a diamond symbol, rather than a bar (since the milestone has no duration).

		Task Name	Duration	May 1, '16 S S M T W T F
0		⊿ **Sell my house**	**60 days**	
1		⊿ **Fix up house to sell**	**5 days**	
2		Paint bedrooms & Family Room	5 days	
3		Replace carpeting	5 days	
4		Repair roof	1 day	
5		Fix up completed	0 days	◆ 5/2
6		⊿ **Clean up House**	**5 days**	
7		Clean out storage space	5 days	
8		Clean up house	5 days	
9		Hold garage sale	2 days	
10		Clean up completed	0 days	◆ 5/2
11		⊿ **Hire Realtor**	**5 days**	
12		Interview several realtors	5 days	
13		Review contract	3 days	
14		Realtor Hired	0 days	◆ 5/2

Figure 4-27   In this view tasks 5, 10 and 14 are milestones. They have a zero duration and a milestone icon on the Gantt chart.

Manual vs Automatic

Project 2013 provides two scheduling methods for creating project schedules. The methods are the traditional or automatic scheduling and manual scheduling.

Traditional or Automatic Scheduling

This scheduling method was used in prior versions of Microsoft Project and is contained in Project 2013. After tasks are entered relationships or dependencies are created between the tasks. The task durations with their relationships established the timeline for the schedule. This scheduling method allows for bottom up scheduling where the sum of the detail tasks establishes the timeline for the project.

Manual Scheduling

Manual scheduling allows for top-down scheduling where summary tasks may be added first and the details of the project work is completed later. It also permits more unknowns during the scheduling process and the ability to complete the details when known. Tasks do not have to contain relationships and dates or freeform text may be entered.

Project scheduling mode will be selected on a task by task basis. Manually scheduled tasks and automatic scheduled tasks may be mixed within the same project schedule. Each task will contain a column called task mode which will establish the scheduling mode assigned to a task.

When to Use Manual vs. Automatic Scheduling

Manual vs. automatic scheduling usage will deliver very different results. The amount of information concerning the project that is available to the scheduler when the schedule is created might lend the scheduler to select one method over the other when creating the initial schedule. It may be advantageous to use both scheduling methods within a schedule switching between scheduling methods when needed.

Use Manual Scheduling When

- Minimal information is available about the project and you need to put your ideas (tasks and durations) into an initial schedule.
- Tasks are assigned to specific dates and you are not comfortable with the schedule moving as other tasks are entered or as resources are assigned.
- Using top-down planning – entering duration values for summary tasks followed by detail tasks and milestones to complete the work of the summary tasks.
- Using free form planning of tasks and durations to produce a Gantt chart.
- Need to build a rough schedule for a future project
- Relationships between tasks are not known.

Use Automatic Scheduling When

- More complete information is known about the goals of the project.
- Using bottom up planning. Enter the summary tasks and create the WBS structure. The detail tasks within the summaries will calculate the duration of the summary tasks.

- You want the schedule to be dynamic. Tasks will be adjusted reacting to changes within the schedule.
- You want the scheduling engine to calculate dates in the schedule.
- Resource allocations, resource assignments based on hours, earned value analysis or more accurate metrics are needed.

Consider Using a Combination of Both Methods When

- Initial planning may be in manual mode. As decisions are made and more detail is known, tasks may be converted to automatic mode.
- Consider converting to automatic mode when project execution begins. This may be done for the entire project, by phase or range of tasks.

Change to Auto Schedule

The column or field in Project 2013 that determines which scheduling mode a task is in is called "Task Mode". By default, you will see this field on the Entry table of the Gantt Chart. This column may be added to any task table.

Setting the automatic or manual scheduling mode may be accomplished in several ways:

To set the scheduling mode for a project or for all future projects:

- **File → Options → Schedule**
- Choose the option from **Scheduling options for this project**
- Choose the option from **New tasks created**

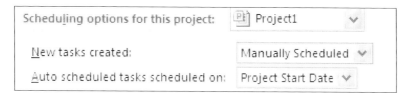

Figure 4-28   Task Schedule Options from the Project Options Dialog Box.

After several tasks are entered you may decide to switch to a different scheduling mode for the addition of future tasks for the project. This can be done quickly using the option at the bottom left hand corner of the Gantt Chart view which is shown below. Changing this option will not affect existing tasks in the schedule; it will only affect future added tasks. Click on the button highlighted below for the option to change scheduling modes:

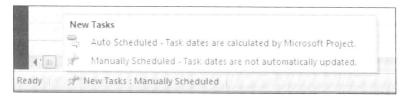

Figure 4-29   Task Schedule Options from the Status Bar.

The default Entry Table for the Gantt Chart includes the "Task Mode" column inserted to the left of the Task Name column. This column may be inserted into any table as needed. The indicators in this column indicate the scheduling mode for the task. In the view below the automatically scheduled tasks have a Gantt bar with an arrow icon and the manually scheduled tasks have a push pin icon in the Task Mode column. Hover your mouse pointer over the icon and the scheduling mode description will appear. Clicking on the arrow next to the icon will allow for scheduling mode changes per task. Note the different Gantt bar formats for manual v automatically scheduled tasks.

		Task Mode	Task Name	Duration	30, '12	Jan 6, '13
0			Commercial Construction 2010 tracking	346 days		
1			Three-story Office Building (76,000 square feet)	346 days		
2			General Conditions	8 days		
3			Receive notice to proceed and sign contract	3 days		
4			Submit bond and insurance documents	1 day		
5			Prepare and submit project schedule	2.8 days		
6			Prepare and submit schedule of values	2 days		
7			Obtain building permits	4 days		
8			Submit preliminary shop drawings	1 wk		
9			Submit monthly requests for payment	1 day		

Figure 4-30   Gantt Chart View Showing the Task Mode Column in the Entry Table.

To change the scheduling mode from the Task tab:

- Click the task to be changed
- Click **Task → Manual Schedule or Automatic Schedule**

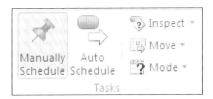

Figure 4-31   Task Schedule Options from the Task Tab on the Ribbon.

Another way to change the scheduling mode is to double click a task to open the Task Information dialog box. An option is located on the General tab to change the scheduling mode. The options are highlighted in the view below.

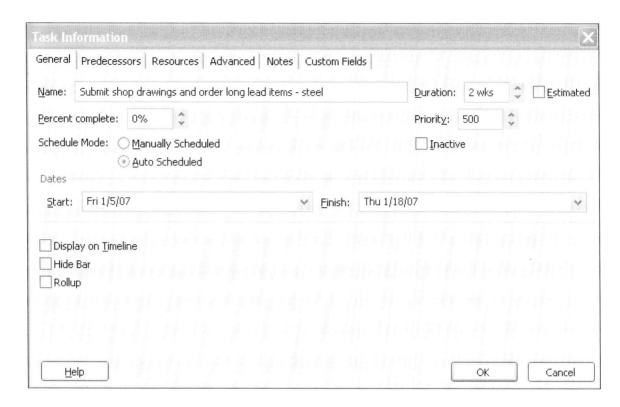

Figure 4-32   Task Schedule Options from the Task Information Dialog Box.

Key Points to Remember

- Project is capable of handling any scheduling methodology, not just traditional waterfall. You can also use a combination of approaches within one schedule such as Waterfall with an Agile component.
- Organizing your schedule hierarchically into a Work Breakdown Structure (WBS) can assist with reporting to management and schedule maintenance.
- Use 5 or less outline levels in your WBS.
- Custom WBS numbers allow you to create a code for each task that does not match the outline numbers built-in to Project.
- Consider following a naming approach and structure to each section in your schedule for consistency across projects.
- Use milestones to capture goals and give them a duration of 0.
- Selecting the task number (ID) is a best practice before inserting, deleting, moving, or copying a task.
- Use manual and automatic scheduling where appropriate to give control of the task planning to the scheduler or project manager.

A D V I S I C O N®

Chapter 5

Estimating, Linking, and Lead & Lag

"If we are to replace standard numerical probability usage with engineering judgment, why do we find such an enormous disparity between the management estimate and the judgment of the engineers? It would appear that, for whatever purpose, be it for internal or external consumption, the management of NASA exaggerates the reliability of its product, to the point of fantasy."

~ Richard Feynman

Overview

A somewhat time consuming but critical aspect of scheduling is the estimating process. During this process you need to decide if you are doing a top down or bottom up approach and where you will get your estimates from. Planning for task estimates and resource estimates will be required along with learning more about how Project's scheduling engine uses your estimates in its calculations.

The next logical step would be sequencing of activities which is controlled by task dependencies and linking features. You need to become familiar with the four types and how they can be tailored with lag and lead time. If there is an opportunity to disable tasks at a point in time, the inactivate feature can also be applied.

Overview of Estimating

Estimating is the ability to make an educated guess as to the duration, and work of a task. Project Management is both an art and a science. Estimating task durations and work draws on the project manager's skills and experience during the estimation process. Estimates take into consideration factors such as resource skill, history, and experience. In this lesson we take a look at estimating duration and work.

How Project 2013 Defines and Calculates Work and Duration

It would be helpful to understand the formula that will be driving the scheduling of the tasks before you enter your estimates:

Work = Duration * Units (quantity of a resource)

OR

Duration = Work / Units (quantity of a resource)

Estimating Techniques

- **Top down estimating**: used when performing the same types of projects frequently. Top-down estimating allows for estimating the length of a phase. The details for tasks will follow. Manual scheduling mode in Project 2013 allows for this type of estimating model. You can use this method when you do not have a lot of information about the project but would like to start getting something down while working toward a project schedule.
- **Bottom up estimating**: estimating each task work package or deliverable of the project (this could be at the task level) will allow for the accumulated roll up of the values to create the length of the project. The roll up will accumulate at the summary task levels as totals for duration, work and cost. In turn, the summary tasks will roll up to the project summary task for a grand total for the project.

What to Estimate?

- Estimate duration (length of time) in minutes, hours, days, months, etc.
- Estimate work (amount of work) in minutes, hours, days, months, etc.
- Estimate duration and work in minutes, hours, days, months, etc.

To create consistency within an organization it is recommended that an estimating standard be established. Most schedulers estimate work in hours and duration in days. Longer projects might be estimated using work in days and duration is weeks. Having a standard will help create a consistency across an organization.

Where Do the Estimates Come From?

Estimates may come from the project manager, team members, subject matter experts, stakeholders, historic data, experience, etc.

How Do You Get Good Estimates?

Ask the right people: look for the most experienced person in a specific skill area. Chances are, they have worked a project similar to or have actually performed the work in the past. These types of people can be invaluable to a project manager for estimating.

Ask the performing resource: if you are lucky enough to know who your resources will be for the project, the performing resource is always the best source for an estimate. However, how you ask the resource for the estimate will make a difference. If you ask for an estimate, most people are thinking about fitting the work into their current workload. Framing the question from the point of view that the project will be worked some time in the future will result in a more accurate response. They should only consider how long (or how much work) it would take to perform the task regardless of the specific timeframe.

Subject Matter Experts: always a good source for advice.

Padding, slack, and time reserve should be included in any schedule. Every organization and project management methodology has its own approach. The important point is that extra time should be built into all schedules to help manage the inevitable contingencies that will occur during the performance of all projects. If padding, slack or time reserves are not included in the planning, the schedule will not be realistic and will result in a reduced probability of completing the project as planned.

If the work is increased to allow for contingencies, the cost will also increase. Consider increasing duration which will extend the length of time and not necessarily effect cost.

Estimating for Unknown Resources

Most project managers plan the work for a project and find out what specific resources will perform the tasks in the future. Tasks might require a specific skill level but the quality of the unfamiliar resource is unknown. How do you plan for unknown resources?

When estimating tasks, consider estimating a task for a senior level resource or a junior level resource:

- The senior level person would accomplish the task faster and would cost more.
- The junior level resource would cost less but needs more time and training.

Outsourcing resources: although there is a quantity of highly qualified contract resources, the recommendation is to estimate these tasks at the junior level. You will need to account for a learning curve, assimilation into your organization and ramp up time. The project manager might request a specific skill level but it is unknown whether or not that skill will be available when the project requires it.

Entering Estimates

The Entry table of the Gantt chart is designed for easy entry of task estimates. Adding the Work column to the view will enable adding work estimates.

To insert the Work column in to the Entry table of the Gantt Chart view:

1. **Tasks → Gantt Chart** (the default value will be the Entry table)
2. Right click on the column heading **Start**
3. Select **Insert Column**
4. Click on the "W" key on the keyboard
5. Click on **Work**

For each task enter one of the following:

- A duration value
- A work value
- A duration and a work value

Valid entry values:

- 1m = 1 minute
- 1h = 1 hour
- 1d = 1 day
- 1w = 1 week
- 1mo = 1 month
- 1 y = 1 year

Abbreviations of the time values may be customized in the Schedule options:

File → Options → Advanced → Display options for this project

Duration entries will be scheduled as work days as defined by the project calendar.

Physical days (actual day count including non-working days) may also be achieved by using the **Elapsed** time. By placing an "E" in front of the letter in the duration field, the value will be scheduled in physical number of days. For example: 13 ed = 13 physical days.

In the example below note:

- Task 1 – 5 business days
- Task 2 – 1 day, 40 hours of work
- Task 3 – 5 days, 20 hours of work
- Task 4 – 5 edays – elapsed time or physical days

Note the scheduling difference:

Task Name	Duration	Work					Jun 5, 16				
			W	T	F	S	S	M	T	W	T
Task 1	5 days	0 hrs									
Task 2	1 day?	40 hrs									
Task 3	5 days	20 hrs									
Task 4	5 edays	0 hrs									

Figure 5-1   After inserting the Work column into the table, enter Duration, Work or Duration and Work.

Other helpful information:

- When task durations are entered, a "?" will be added within the duration field. This "?" represents that the task information has not been finalized and is considered estimated. This indicator is optional and may be turned off at **File → Options → Schedule** and un-checking the following options:
  - Show that scheduled tasks have estimated durations
  - New scheduled tasks have estimated durations
- Manual scheduling mode for a task has the benefit of not requiring values in duration, start and finish columns. Text may be added as a note to the scheduler. If the task mode is changed to automatic scheduling, the text will be lost and, the software will enter a valid value. Scheduling modes are discussed in *Manual vs Automatic* on page 120. In the view below note the values in the duration, start and finish columns for Task 5:

5	⚑?	Task 5	ask Bob	0 hrs	mid-June	mid-July	
6	⬛	Task 6	1 day?	0 hrs	6/2/16	6/2/16	

Figure 5-2   Task 5 is an example of a Manual Scheduled task. Task 6 is an Automatic scheduled task.

Inserting **Effort-driven** and **Type** columns will allow for setting these values for each task as well. As discussed in *Options* on page 75, each task will be unique in the nature of the work to be performed. As a result, these settings should be adjusted to determine what task type and effort-driven values are appropriate for a task.

Concept of the Scheduling Engine

Dynamic scheduling is the use of task relationships and dependencies to drive the sequence and ultimately the timing of the schedule. Project's scheduling engine supports dynamic scheduling in automatic scheduling mode.

This means that as the project progresses and you make adjustments to tasks, Project automatically recalculates the effect on subsequent tasks. This will also show the project manager if the overall schedule is extended and provide analysis opportunity to monitor if the change creates multiple critical paths, potential resource constraints, and so on.

Project will also highlight those tasks affected by a change so the project manager can easily see the ripple effect of the current proposed task changes. Project 2013 can aid the scheduler in exploring alternate scenarios as a what-if analysis.

If constraints (which will be discussed in *Constraints* on page 163) are utilized to lock in task dates, the dates will disable Project's built-in scheduling engine and a project manager will not be able to see the effects downstream in the schedule. Maintaining this dynamic visibility is vital in effectively and pro-actively managing a schedule. This is why it is a best practice to not use constraints, unless necessary and appropriate to.

Sequencing

Project 2013 calculates the duration of a project based on task durations and how task dependencies are created between tasks. Establishing the order of the tasks is called Sequencing. Sequencing is concerned with establishing the order tasks should or could be performed. Arranging tasks in the most efficient order for the project is not an easy exercise. Sometimes, the order of the tasks is very evident and at other times, more complicated. The task sequencing order is up to the scheduler and needs to be focused on what is right for a specific project.

For example, the following tasks are tasks that someone would do when they come home after work and before they go to bed:

1. Arrive Home
2. Eat Dinner
3. Walk the dog
4. Run an errand
5. Read the mail
6. Clean up the dinner dishes
7. Cook dinner
8. Go to Sleep
9. Get the mail
10. Watch the news

Take a minute to write down the numbers of the tasks above in the order you would perform these tasks. If you have some post-it notes you can write the task names on the notes and move the notes around to achieve the sequencing order.

Did you notice that some tasks have a forced relationship?

- You can't eat dinner until you have cooked dinner.
- You can't read the mail until you get the mail.

Other relationships will work in a more random order:

- Run the errand.
- Watch the news.

Try this exercise again taking into consideration that you have a second person helping you achieve these tasks.

What you might have noticed this time you sequenced the tasks:

- The project took a shorter length of time.
- The work was divided over the workers.
- Some tasks were performed with the people working together and others were performed by only one worker.

Compare your task list to others in the class. You might see that the work will get done but others have a different opinion as to the order the tasks will be completed. Is one list more right than another list?

What you are seeing is the art of project management. Projecting what will work best for a given situation is derived from experience, opinion and the workers performing the tasks. Project provides task relationships to support task sequencing which is discussed in the next section.

Creating Task Dependencies

Once the tasks are entered into the project schedule, the next step is to consider in what order the tasks should be performed. Many tasks will have a flexible order and others will have a forced order of performance. Establishing the order of the tasks is one of the factors that will help calculate the timeline of the project schedule. A dependency is the name given to the relationship established between the tasks used to establish the order of tasks. If dependencies are not created, Project 2013 will not be able to accurately predict and adjust dependent future tasks based on completed work.

Task Dependency Types

Project 2013 allows for 4 types of task dependencies. These dependencies establish the order that the tasks will be performed. Dependencies may also be referred to as links, relationships or relationships between tasks. The result of creating task relationships is a network of related tasks establishing a time line. When referring to linked tasks the following terms will apply:

- A task that has a relationship directly before a task is known as a predecessor task
- A task that has a relationship directly after a task is known as a successor task

In the view below there are 4 tasks. The relationships are established as link lines between tasks.

- The predecessor task or task that comes before is the "Paint bedrooms and Family Room" task.

- The successor task or task that comes after the "Replace carpeting" task is the "Repair roof" task.

Pointing to a link line between tasks will display information regarding the task relationship. Notice the pop-up information box which shows the details of the relationship between the "Repair roof" task and the "Fix up completed" task.

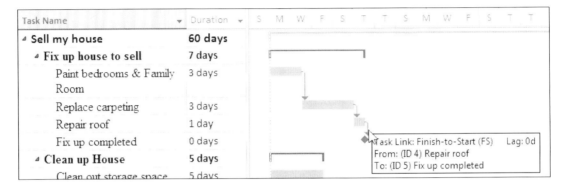

Figure 5-3   View of linked task dependencies.

Not all dependencies are the same. Some tasks will start at the same time where others might be scheduled one after the other. To facilitate scheduling needs, there are 4 dependency types which are:

- Finish-to-start
- Start-to-start
- Finish-to-finish
- Start-to-finish

The details of each of the relationship types is described below:

- Finish-to-Start (FS)
  - Default dependency for the Project 2013
  - Task 1 must complete before Task 2 can begin
  - This relationship type creates a waterfall effect
    - Example: Drive to the restaurant, then eat dinner
      Build a wall then paint the wall

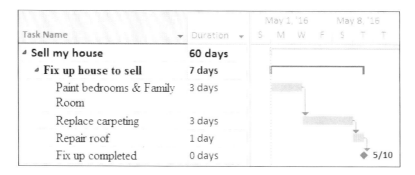

Figure 5-4   This is an example of a Finish-to-Start relationship.

- Start-to-Start (SS)
    - Tasks that are scheduled to start at the same time
        - Example: You can start to clean out the Storage space at the same time you have the painters painting the bedroom and family room.

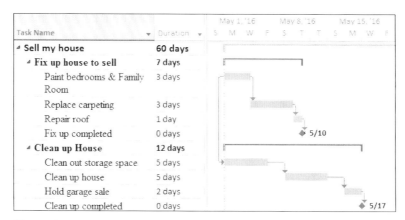

Figure 5-5   Tasks Paint bedrooms & Family room is related Start-to-Start with Clean out storage space.

- Finish-to-Finish (FF)
    - Tasks that are scheduled to finish at the same time but not required to start at the same time.
        - Example: The section of work below can all start when the previous section is completed. These tasks will start at different times, but they all need to be completed by the same point in time.

⊿ Clean up House	5 days	0 hrs	
Clean out storage space	5 days	0 hrs	
Clean up house	5 days	0 hrs	
Hold garage sale	2 days	0 hrs	
Clean up completed	0 days	0 hrs	5/6

Figure 5-6   The tasks above are in a Finish-to-Finish relationship.

- Start-to-Finish (SF)
  - The start date of the predecessor task will determine the finish date of the successor task.
  - This is the least used dependency type.
  - Example: When the new software module comes on line, the old software will be taken off line

House on the market	60 days	0 hrs	
Review contracts	2 days	0 hrs	
House Sold	0 days	0 hrs	7/26
Move into new house	5 days	0 hrs	

Figure 5-7   Example of Start-to-Finish relationship.

Task Relationships and Manually Scheduled Tasks

When working with manually scheduled tasks, errors might result using dependencies. A warning is displayed when tasks are linked and dates are entered into the start or finish columns. The calculation of the project duration might not match the duration calculated when the entered dates are taken into consideration. *Figure 5-8* is an example of an error created when the duration entered for a manually scheduled summary task is smaller than the sum of the detail tasks contained in the summary grouping. Note the bar below the summary task brackets is longer than the brackets and there are dots around the Gantt bar for the House on the market task. There are also squiggly lines under the Finish dates for several tasks.

Add the File Creating and Modifying Dependency Types

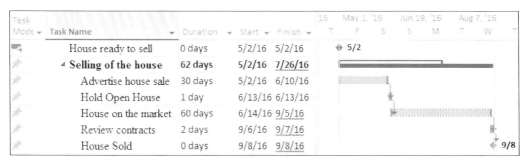

Figure 5-8   Manually scheduled tasks displaying error message.

To correct this type of error, Project 2013 has a feature called Task Inspector. Right click on the red error line and the following choices appear. Select the Fix in Task Inspector option and correction choices are displayed.

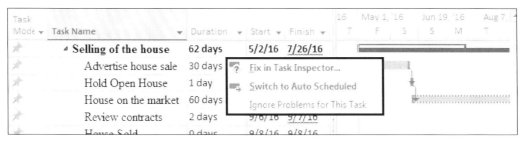

Figure 5-9   Error displayed on Manually scheduled task. Right click on error to display resolution options.

Below is the result of clicking on the Fix in Task Inspector option for the task. Note the error message is no longer visible and the task in error has been rescheduled.

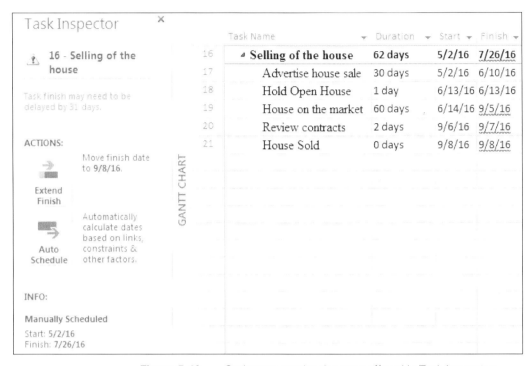

Figure 5-10   Options to resolve the error offered in Task Inspector.

Task Inspector will be discussed in *Methods for Resolving Resource Conflicts* on page 252.

Best Practices for Using Dependencies

Links between tasks will allow you to create a network of related tasks. The network will show the order the tasks will occur. Below are some best practices which should be considered when creating relationships:

- All tasks should have both a predecessor and a successor. The timeline for the project is based on task duration and relationships. If tasks are not linked in the network of tasks, their duration will not be accounted for within the timeline. Making sure all tasks are included will avoid surprises at the end of a project.

- When creating dependencies or relationships, apply the rule – *because I can, is it a good idea?* Do not link every task to every other task.
- Think about what task pushes or influences another task. If a task is late, what other tasks will be affected? Link only tasks with a direct effect on a successor task. Ask yourself what needs to be completed before you can do the next step and if it is late, which tasks will be affected.
- Link detail tasks and milestones only. The completion of tasks will push the milestones or the short term goals. Linking summary tasks means that an entire section of work must be completed before the next section may be started. Ask yourself if that is true for your situation before linking at the summary level. Linking summary tasks is not recommended.
- Tasks should always be linked to push milestones. For example: define what the definition of "project completed" is. If multiple parallel paths must be completed to conclude the project, they should all be linked to the ending milestone. If any of the parallel paths takes longer than planned, the milestone date will be pushed out in time.

In the example below "Paint bedrooms & Family Room" is the starting task for the project. All 3 sections of work can start when the project starts. All 3 sections must be completed before the house is ready to sell. If any of the sections take longer, each section has the ability to push the ending milestone or when the house is ready to sell. The longest of the parallel paths will be considered the critical path or the project section that determines the timeline of the project.

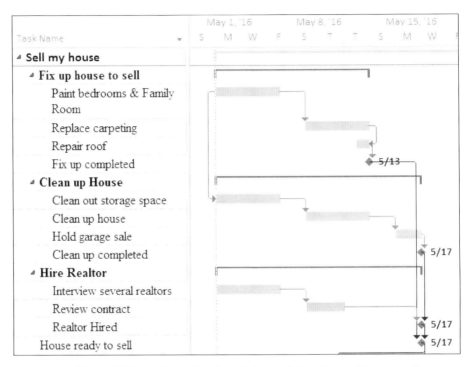

Figure 5-11   Example of multiple parallel paths pushing an ending milestone.

- Create as many parallel paths as possible to shorten the schedule. Use of the Start-To-Start and Finish-To–Finish relationships will help create parallel paths and shorten the project time line. Be aware, however, just because you can schedule tasks in parallel, you might not have the resources to perform the work which could result in extending the timeline.

- Do not link tasks based on a resource. Some people will plan tasks to occur at specific times because they think that a resource will be available at that time. Chances are the expected resources will not be available at the planned point in time because other tasks for that resource have changed. Plan the schedule for the work required and plan/arrange for required resources as the time draws nearer to when the task will be performed.

- Links may be external to the project. Project 2013 will allow dependencies to exist in other projects that are linked to tasks in your project. This is similar to links in Excel. In Excel, if links between files are cre-

©2014 Advisicon, Inc.

ated and the files are relocated, the links will be broken. Project 2013's links between project files will work the same way.

Project 2013 also offers the option for tasks that are moved or added within the schedule to automatically link in a Finish-to-Start relationship or not be linked at all. This is a personal preference and may be applied to a specific project or all projects viewed on your desktop.

To view or change this option: **File → Options → Schedule**

Scheduling options for this project: ▣ Sell my house - ex4.mpp ▼

New tasks created: Auto Scheduled ▼

Auto scheduled tasks scheduled on: Project Start Date ▼

Duration is entered in: Days ▼

Work is entered in: Hours ▼

Default task type: Fixed Units ▼

☐ New tasks are effort driven ⓘ   ☑ Tasks will always honor their constraint dates ⓘ

☑ Autolink inserted or moved tasks ⓘ   ☑ Show that scheduled tasks have estimated durations ⓘ

☑ Split in-progress tasks ⓘ   ☑ New scheduled tasks have estimated durations

☑ Update Manually Scheduled tasks when editing links   ☐ Keep task on nearest working day when changing to Automatically Scheduled mode

Figure 5-12   Scheduling options.

Lead & Lag

Relationships between tasks are not always absolutely defined as described with relationships. Allowing for Lead and Lag time will help refine a schedule to bring it more in line with the actual timeline for the project. Lead and Lag time will allow for wait time between tasks and overlap of task activities.

In this section we will discuss:

1. What is Lag time?
2. What is Lead time?
3. Best Practices for using Lead and Lag time

What is Lag Time?

Lag time is used to provide wait time between tasks. The time will be expressed in business days or specified project calendar working days. Lag time should be used to extend the timeline of the project when only duration needs to be added to a schedule and you will not add work or cost. For example: New concrete is poured and you must wait 6 days before you can drive on it. The time must occur but no work or cost is added to the task. A dependency must first exist between tasks before Lag time can be created.

To create Lag time:

Double click the relationship line between tasks where you would like to add the lag time. The task dependency dialog box below will appear. In *Figure 5-13*, there are 2 tasks. After the Paint bedrooms and Family Room task is completed you decide that you would like to wait 3 days for the paint to dry before Replacing the Carpeting.

To add Lag time between tasks:

1. Double click on the link line between tasks. The Task Dependency Box
   will be displayed.
2. Add time to the **Lag** box.
3. Click **OK**.

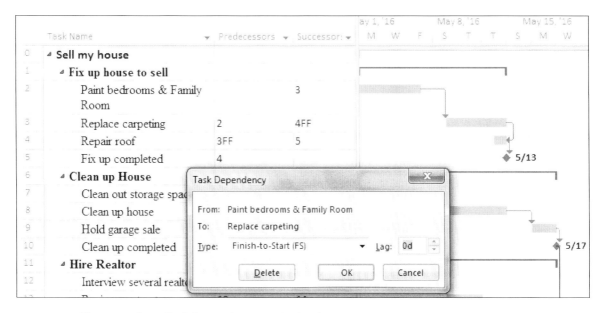

Figure 5-13   Task Dependency box before lag time is added.

The result of adding a 3 day lag is displayed below. Note the values in the
predecessor and successor columns. If you prefer, you can type these
values in and not enter lag using the Task Dependency box.

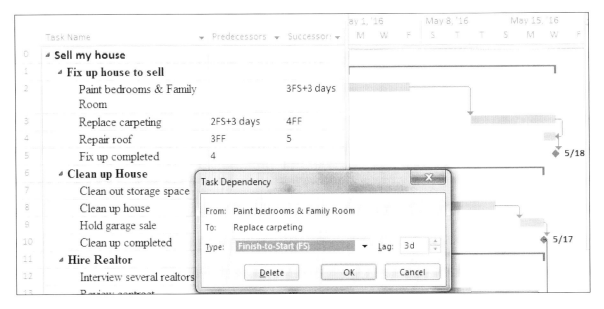

Figure 5-14   Task dependency box with 3 day lag time added.

Lag time may also be expressed as a percentage of the duration of the predecessor task. Order equipment is a 5 day task. 50% Lag would mean that the length of the lag time would be 2.5 days or half of the 5 days duration of the Order equipment task.

What is Lead Time?

Lead time shortens the time line of the project. Consider tasks that do not need to be 100% completed before the successor task can start. Lead time is a good tool to help refine the schedule when trying to cut time from a timeline. Project 2013 does not have a field or box called Lead time. Instead, to create Lead time negative Lag time is entered.

To create Lead time:

The view below is showing that Task 7 "Clean out storage space" should be completed before starting Task 8 "Clean up house." Each task will take 5 days for a total duration of 10 days plus weekend time to complete this work. If other resources were available to help clean the house, this task could start earlier and save total time to complete both tasks.

Below is a view of the tasks before lead time is entered. Note the total duration for the 2 tasks and the milestone ending date of 5/17.

Figure 5-15   Tasks without Lead time.

To enter Lead time between two tasks:

Double click the relationship line between tasks where lead time is to be added.

Enter "–3d" in the Lag field value

Click **OK** to close the box

Below is the result of adding lead time between two tasks. Note the overlap of tasks and the total scheduling time has been shortened. Note the value in the predecessor column and in the Lag box in the Task Dependency box. Compared to the view without lead time, the milestone for this group of work is now scheduled 5 days sooner.

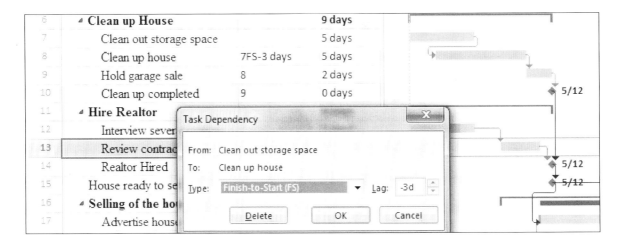

Figure 5-16   Tasks with Lead time.

Lead time can also be expressed in percentages. The advantage to using percentages is if the predecessor task length changes, the successor task will automatically adjust its starting date.

For example:

- Task A is 10 days long and has a Finish-to-start relationship with Task B with -50% lead time
- Task B will be scheduled to start when Task A has 5 days of work completed
- Task A is taking longer than expected and is now scheduled to take 15 days
- Task B will be rescheduled to start when Task A has 7.5 days of work 7.5 days of work is scheduled to be completed.

A -50% would move the successor task to the left 50% of the duration of the predecessor task. *Figure 5-17* demonstrates the result of applying -50% for Lead time to the relationship between these two tasks.

To enter Lead time between two tasks as a percentage value:

- Double click the relationship line between tasks where lead time is required.
- Enter "–50%" in the Lag field value
- Click **OK** to close the box

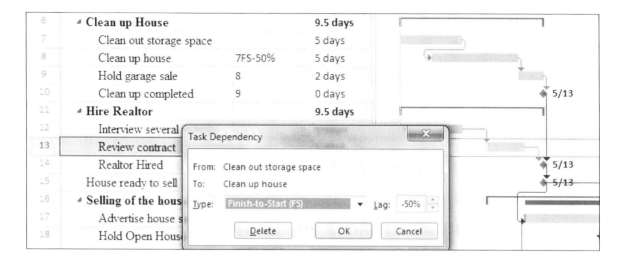

Figure 5-17 Lead time entered in a percentage.

Best Practices Using Lead and Lag Time

Best practices for the use of **Lag** time in a project schedule. Add Lag time when:

- Time must go by without a work or cost applied to the time. Lag is considered to be wait time like a delivery of equipment or concrete hardening.
- You would like to add slack into the schedule to extend the timeline to allow for possible contingencies during project execution.
- You would like to add wait or cushion time between phases of a project
- You would like to add wait time between parallel sections of a project to allow others to catch up.
- Lag time may also be expressed in elapsed time to allow nights and weekends to be included

- Planning the work for a factory crew. For example: the crew needs to be at work for 9 hours but 8 of that is actual work. The remaining hour is meal and breaks. Use Lag to extend the time for the work of the crew to accommodate breaks.

Use lead time when the schedule needs to be shortened. More resources will be needed to accomplish the tasks. Lead time can increase risk of re-work and could increase cost for tasks.

Best practices for the use of **Lead** time in a project schedule:

- Piece work – when X number of items or time has been completed, give the completed work to the next group to start their work.
- Testing – when X percentage of the testing is completed and successful, give the completed work to the next group to start their work.
- When it is not necessary for the predecessor task to achieve 100% completion before starting the successor task.

Inactivate Tasks

When developing a schedule or even after a schedule is being executed, you may have portions of the schedule that may be optional or you may be looking for ways to run a scenario which leaves out a portion of the schedule from the scheduling engine. Choosing to inactivate a collection of tasks is a way to temporarily or permanently remove tasks from the rest of the schedule, but still leave the information about those tasks intact so you can reactivate them at a later time as desired, or keep this inactive data for historical purposes. This feature saves time over having to delete and re-enter task information. All tasks by default are active unless you make them inactive.

This feature is in Project Professional 2013 only.

To inactivate a task:

1. Select the task(s).
2. On the **Task** tab, **Schedule** group, click **Inactivate**.

Figure 5-18   Section of the Task ribbon with Inactivate button.

In *Figure 5-19* all of the tasks are active:

	Task Mode ▾	Task Name ▾	Duration
6		◢ **Clean up House**	**12 days**
7		Clean out storage space	5 days
8		Clean up house	5 days
9		Hold garage sale	2 days
10		Clean up completed	0 days

Figure 5-19   View of active tasks.

It has been decided that the "Clean the House" task is not needed for the project schedule.   In the view below you will see the result of adjusting this task to inactive status. Notice the changes to the schedule. The "Clean up House" task has a line through its name and is shadow formatted. The task bar for the task is clear and the predecessor task has been re-scheduled to accommodate for the inactivated task.

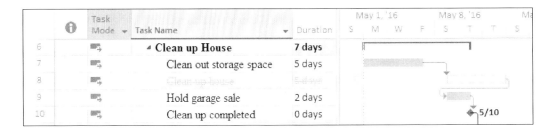

	Task Mode ▾	Task Name ▾	Duration
6		◢ **Clean up House**	**7 days**
7		Clean out storage space	5 days
8		Clean up house	5 days
9		Hold garage sale	2 days
10		Clean up completed	0 days

Figure 5-20   Inactivated tasks.

If you made a mistake and accidentally inactivate the wrong task(s), simply click **Inactivate** again to make them active.

This feature is especially useful when you are struggling with test/retest cycles. Simply inactivate the extra cycles until they are needed.

Inactive tasks are a great way to include contingency actions which only apply if a planned risk actually manifests itself in the future.

Key Points to Remember

- Project applies a formula when scheduling tasks.
- Estimating is done in either a top down or bottom up approach.
- Both task information and resource information is estimated.
- Good estimates come from individuals who perform the work or historical information.
- Project includes a ? symbol in every duration cell where a numeric value has not been actually entered as a reminder.
- Dynamic scheduling means that linked tasks will respond to changes in the schedule as long as the tasks are auto scheduled.
- Sequencing is the concept of putting things in a logical order in your schedule.
- There are four dependency types with Finish to Start as the most common.
- A predecessor is a task which comes before another task in a Finish to Start relationship.
- A successor is the task which comes after another task in a Finish to Start relationship.
- Use only necessary links to establish relationships.
- In a Finish to Start relationship lag time provides for an additional waiting period before the successor task starts.
- In a Finish to Start relationship, lead time provides for an overlap between the two tasks and is entered as a negative number.
- Lead time may be useful when trying to shorten the timeline.
- Inactivate tasks instead of deleting tasks to leave a visual reminder that the tasks are not currently needed in the schedule.

Chapter 6
Constraints and Deadlines

"I love deadlines. I love
the whooshing noise they
make as they go by."

~ Douglas Adams

Overview

Most of us deal with constraints and deadlines in our schedules on a regular basis. In Project these features serve different purposes and are often used incorrectly. We will show you how to keep your schedule as dynamic as possible by teaching you the best way to apply these features.

In some instances, a task cannot be moved. Working around the task with a split might be the best solution. Another way to accommodate a deadline or constraint is to change the scheduled working time for a specific task through a task calendar.

Additional features that are deployed in the everyday management of a schedule include techniques to move a project that is being postponed and adding notes to document reasons for various task situations.

Constraints

As discussed throughout this book, you should take advantage of Project's scheduling features to illustrate schedules that are dynamic and forecast results. However, most organizations want to include restrictions to the schedule that are due to sponsor needs. In this section we will illustrate the occasional need to include a constraint and the benefits and disadvantage of this feature.

What are Constraints?

Constraints are defined as conditions upon which a project must be managed against which can negatively affect budget, quality, schedule and scope.

Some typical constraints might include a lack of:

- Money
- Skilled resources
- Requirements for the project
- Equipment
- Management support
- Time

Even though the above constraints are important to the success of a project, Project 2013 cannot account for all of them. The constraints feature in Project 2013 can specifically help you with date restrictions.

Tasks may require a target date, start at a specific date, end at a specific date, or require scheduling at the beginning or ending of a timeframe.

Date constraints can be used to refine the project schedule when greater control is needed for specific tasks' start or finish dates. Using date constraints, however, will also remove flexibility from the schedule. It is for this reason that the use of constraints be kept to a minimum. Some of the date constraints are more flexible than others available. The flexible constraints will be the most beneficial during scheduling.

Manual Scheduled tasks cannot use constraints. They are used for Auto Scheduled tasks only.

Constraint Types

Constraints are used when a task must be scheduled with a specific date in mind or within a specific time period. When setting constraints, the following pieces of information must be known:

- Constraint type
- Date for the constraint

There are 8 constraint types available in the Project 2013 and all are date dependent:

1. **As Soon As Possible (ASAP)** - default constraint applied to all tasks when a project is scheduled from the project start date. Tasks will be scheduled as early as possible within a timeframe.
2. **As Late As Possible (ALAP)** - default constraint applied to tasks when a project is scheduled from the finish date of the project. Tasks will be scheduled as late as possible within a timeframe.
3. **Finish No Earlier Than (FNET)** - applied to a task that must finish no earlier than a specified date. The constraint date will be applied to the finish date of the task and the task will move forward in time to the date specified for this constraint.
4. **Finish No Later Than (FNLT)** - applied to a task that must finish no later than a specified date. During tracking, tasks will move forward in

the schedule. Tasks with a Finish No Later Than constraint will move forward and stop at the constraint date.

5. **Start No Earlier Than (SNET)** - applied to a task that must start no earlier than a specified date. The constraint date will be applied to the start date of the task and the task will move forward in time to the date specified for this constraint.

6. **Start No Later Than (SNLT)** - applied to a task that must be started by a specified date. During tracking, tasks will move forward in the schedule. Tasks with a Start No Later Than constraint will move forward and stop at the constraint date.

7. **Must Start On** – applied when a task has a hard start date. The task will move to the constraint date and is fixed on that date.

8. **Must Finish On** - applied when a task has a hard finish date. The task will move to the constraint date and is fixed on that date.

To Add a Task Constraint

Add a constraint to indicate a restriction to the overall project schedule, to introduce a new task or task path with a specific starting date, or to introduce a finish restriction on a task.

Preferred Method

Use the Task Information dialog box to ensure you have access to all available options and settings related to the constraint.

1. Double-click any cell in the desired task row to launch Task Information.
2. Click the **Advanced** tab
3. In the **Constraint type** drop-down list, choose the desired constraint
4. In the **Constraint date** field, enter or choose the desired date (optional)
5. Click **OK**

If the planning wizard appears because you are creating a constraint on a task with a link to another task, you must select: **Continue. A XX constraint will be set**. Any of the other choices will alter or cancel the constraint type you selected.

To Remove a Task Constraint

Remove a constraint to allow your project schedule to automatically adjust when changes are introduced. If you receive scheduling errors on a regular basis, you may need to remove some constraints.

Preferred Method

Return the task to its default setting of As Soon As Possible with this method.

1. Double-click any cell in the desired task row to launch Task Information.
2. Click the **Advanced** tab
3. In the **Constraint type** drop-down list, choose **As Soon As Possible**
4. Click **OK**

The Constraint date will be automatically cleared.

As Soon As Possible is for schedules calculated from a Project Start Date.

Fast Method

This method quickly removes a constraint applied to the Start or Finish date.

1. Highlight either the Start or Finish date cell
2. Press the Delete key

This method is typically used when you accidentally enter in the Start or Finish fields.

If you do not have a predecessor link to a task and remove a constraint, the task simply moves to the start of the project and you may lose information related to the desired date for the task. Be sure to create the appropriate links first.

Avoiding Accidental Constraints

The project manager creates constraints when entering a constraint type and date for a task. Constraints can be created in other ways as well, often accidentally.

The most common mistake made in Project is entering dates on auto-scheduled tasks directly in the Entry table portion of the view so that task constraints are created. Unnecessary constraints make it extremely difficult to manage project schedules, and track and update activities within your project.

Constraints on auto-scheduled tasks are set when you do any of the following:

- Enter or select from the date picker pop-up a Start Date directly in the Entry table.
- Enter or select from the date picker pop-up a Finish Date directly in the Entry table.
- Drag a Task Bar in the bar chart left or right.

By setting constraints, you effectively lock those tasks from moving in the future. As your project progress has an ebb and flow of activity that takes the timeline forward or backward, these tasks will remain unmoved and unmovable, and will tend to bring up error messages.

If a Start date is entered for an Automatically scheduled task, a **Start No Earlier Than** constraint will be applied to the task. If a finish date is entered a **Finish No Earlier Than** constraint will be applied.

When working with constraints you may be prompted with a Planning Wizard message. These messages are optional can be turned off individually or globally as desired.

How to Disable the Planning Wizard Messages

As you become more experienced with Project, you might find a need to turn off messages that give shortcuts or advice while you are working. There are two approaches to disabling these messages: disabling individual messages and disabling all messages.

Disable an Individual Message

Use this method to turn off a single message when it appears. This approach allows you to review each message before disabling it.

1. In the Planning Wizard dialog box that appears, click **Don't tell me about this again**.

Disable All Messages

Use this approach to globally control Planning Wizard messages.

1. Click the **File** tab
2. Click **Options**
3. Click **Advanced** in the Project Options dialog box
4. Uncheck **Advice from Planning Wizard**

You can also use this process to enable groups of messages that you individually disabled.

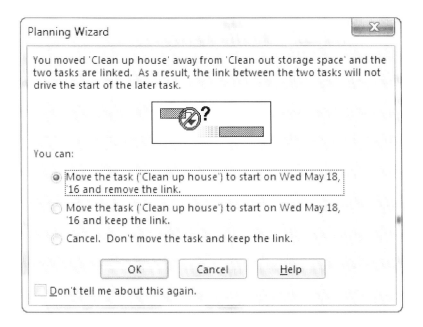

Figure 6-1   Planning Wizard Message.

If Planning Wizard messages are turned off, you will not be alerted to possible scheduling errors that might be created as a result of creating a constraint or other scheduling issues.

You may also notice smart tags appearing in cells as you work with constraints. You may click the drop-down arrow next to the caution indicator to review available options.

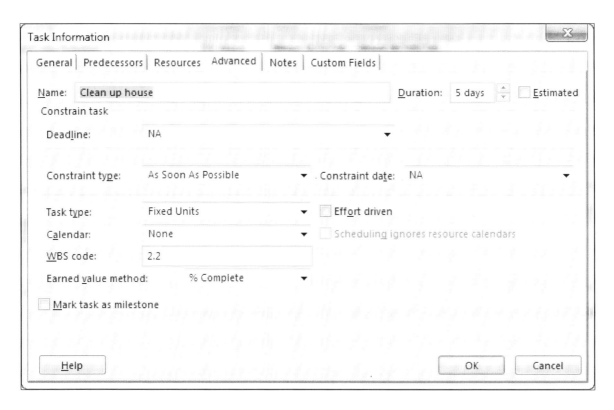

Figure 6-2   Smart Tag Pop-Up.

Selecting an option (even the suggested one by Microsoft Project) may alter your previously applied constraint.

If your scheduling style is to enter dates on each task, it is recommended that you use a manual scheduling approach instead of automatic scheduling. This will allow for tasks to be scheduled to the dates entered and will not be subject to the automatic scheduling engine of the software. If a task is scheduled using manual scheduling, the task can be changed to automatic scheduling at any time.

Constraints may be created as a result of the tracking process. Learn more about this in the *"Rescheduling/Moving a Task"* section of Chapter 10, *Baseline and Tracking*.

Effects of Constraints

Constraints may cause errors in the scheduling of a project that are not readily apparent. Refer to the example below.

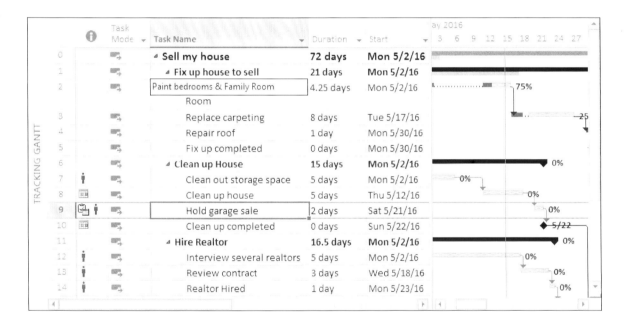

Figure 6-3   Constraint Displayed in Gantt Chart View.

There is an error in the calculation of the date for the task 9 "Initial Planning Complete". The relationship line after task 8, "Selection of Internal Auditors" flows backwards in time. The reason for this is that task 8 is scheduled to complete on April 17, one day later than the milestone target date of April 16. Tasks that are dependent on task 9 will also be miscalculated.

Monitoring for date calculation errors in your schedule is important.

Constraints should be used sparingly and the reason for a constraint should be documented.

If you feel you must use constraints or enter start or finish dates for most of your tasks, manual scheduling might be your scheduling style.

Deadlines

An alternative to a constraint is a deadline which is a great way to include a restriction from the sponsor without changing how the schedule is calculated in Gantt Chart view. Deadlines should be used more frequently than constraints. In this section you will learn how to use deadlines as a warning system for your schedule.

Task Deadlines

Deadlines represent a finish date goal or objective for a task. Using a deadline on a task will still allow it to flow with changes to the schedule and will not restrict its start or finish date like a constraint will.

Use deadlines over constraints to eliminate pop-up error messages when planning or executing your schedule.

A project manager should use deadlines to mark targets in the schedule and to provide simple visual cues when a deadline is missed.

To set a Task Deadline:

1. Double-click any cell in the desired task row to launch Task Information.
2. Click the **Advanced** tab.
3. In the **Deadline field**, choose or enter the desired date.
4. Click **OK**.

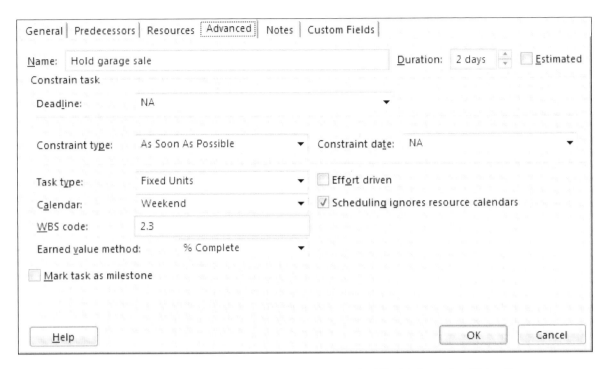

Figure 6-4   Advanced tab of Task Information Dialog Box.

Refer to the following scenarios to further understand deadlines.

A deadline of April 23, 2013 has been assigned to the "Scope Complete" task below. The deadline is represented by the green arrow on the Gantt Chart and does not appear in the Indicator column.

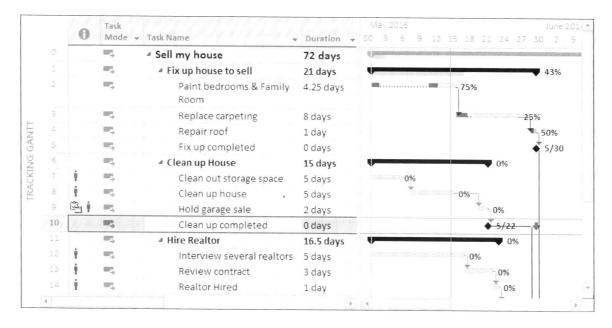

Figure 6-5   Deadline Displayed in Gantt Chart View.

During project execution and tracking of the schedule, tasks will move forward in time. If a task with a deadline moves beyond the deadline arrow, the task will be considered late. Below is an example of the warning that will appear in the Indicator column if a deadline is not met. Notice the red diamond in the indicator column explaining that the task date has exceeded the deadline date.

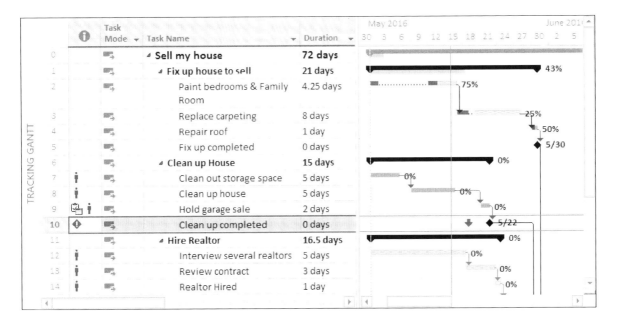

Figure 6-6   Missed Deadline Indicator and Pop-Up in Gantt Chart View.

Another indicator to watch would be the Total Slack column. A negative value indicates that tasks are late and have missed or exceeded the deadline. The negative value indicates how many days the deadline was missed by. It is also an indicator of the amount of recovery time required to get the project back on track.

The Total Slack field provides information on auto scheduled tasks.

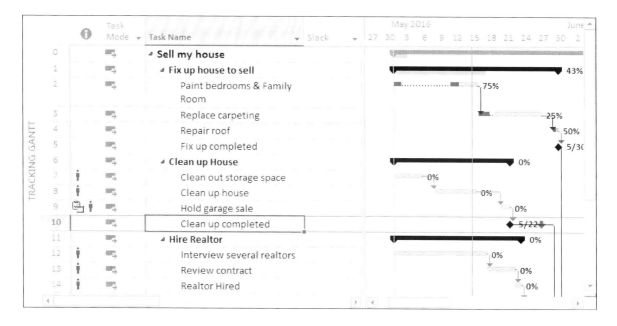

Figure 6-7   Total Slack Field in Gantt Chart View.

Unlike constraints, deadlines do not create date calculation errors in the schedule. Instead, they provide a visual indicator which flags you when deadline targets are missed.

> Deadlines can be used in both manual and automatic scheduling mode.

To remove a Task Deadline

1. Double-click any cell in the desired task row to launch Task Information.
2. Click the **Advanced** tab.
3. In the **Deadline field**, select the date and press Delete.
4. Click **OK**.

> Substitute deadlines for constraints when possible.

Place deadlines on milestones to help manage short term goals. As long as the deadlines stay on the left side of the milestones, you are doing well.

If a deadline date has been exceeded, check the Total Slack column or indicators column on auto scheduled tasks to see how much time needs to be made up to get back on schedule.

Split Tasks

Project's scheduling flexibility includes an option to divide a task into sections to represent various business scenarios. These sections are called splits. In this section, you will learn how to create a split and when it might be used.

Splitting Tasks

There will be times during project scheduling that will require an interruption of work for a particular task. For example when planning a task, some of the work will occur on Monday and the remainder will occur on Monday the following week. In this situation two tasks could be entered or creating a split task would also work. Split tasks are designed for scheduling tasks that start then stop and start again.

When to use split tasks:

- When the work of a long task is required to work around other tasks. Some of the work would be done before a hard date and the remaining portion of the work would be scheduled after the hard date.
- Splits tasks may be used to help even out the resource work load
- 100% of the work for a task is not required to be performed without interruption and could be broken up over time.

To split a Task:

1. Click the Task tab
2. Click the Split Task icon
3. Position the mouse pointer in the middle of the Gantt bar for the desired task
4. Click and drag to the right until the desired split is achieved

Figure 6-8   Link the Selected Tasks Icon.

Refer to the following tips and guidelines regarding task splitting.

Repeat the above steps to create additional splits.

Both auto and manually scheduled tasks can be split.

- Hover the split task mouse pointer over the Gantt bar of the task to be split.

    The screen below will show the information box that will appear.
- As the mouse pointer is dragged the length of the Gantt bar, the date will change in the box. Clicking the mouse pointer will split the task and leave a gap between tasks.

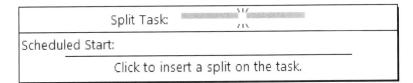

Figure 6-9   Split Task Pop-Up Box.

If the schedule has used "day" durations of tasks as the default scheduling increment, the gap in the split task will advance in 1 day increments or 1 week increments if "weeks" was used. A split task is shown in the view below.

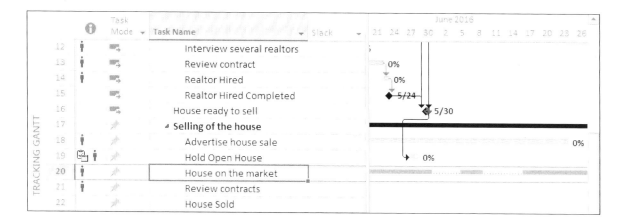

Figure 6-10 Task Split Into Multiple Pieces in Gantt Chart View.

The dots between the sections of the task are the split task indicators showing that the task has been split. The individual parts may be dragged back and forth as necessary to achieve timeframes that will work best for the task. Drag the pieces back together to eliminate the split for the task.

To unsplit a Task:

1. Position the mouse pointer on the left side of a right most bar segment
2. Drag the segment to the left until it connects to the bar segment

> Repeat the above steps to reconnect additional segments if needed.

There are a few rules, however that you should be aware of when working with split tasks:

- When a task is split, it is still one task and will be treated as such.
- Relationships will be applied to the beginning and ending of the entire split tasks only and not to the individual pieces. The individual parts are not separate tasks and cannot have discrete relationships.
- When resources are assigned, the work will be distributed over the total task duration and task as a whole.

- Constraints are applied to the start or the finish of the entire task and cannot be applied to the individual parts.
- The parts of the task may be dragged back together when needed.
- Tasks may be split multiple times.
- Splitting will refine the workload and the duration of the task.

Hiding bar splits will conceal separations of a task and may create confusion when the task duration does not match the Gantt bar length of the task.

Split bars will occur during the tracking process to represent a task which stopped and restarted or a period of inactivity.

Task Calendar

As discovered earlier in this book, Project uses calendars to schedule a task on the timeline and take into account corporate holidays. In this section, you will learn about another use for calendars to control the scheduling of a specific task.

Applying Task Calendars

There will be times when a task must occur within a unique timeframe and outside of the project calendar parameters. In order to accommodate such instances, users can create a distinctive calendar that can be assigned to a task. In doing so the task will be scheduled in the unique timeframe and not affect the scheduling of the entire project.

Below are some examples of when a task calendar would be used:

- Testing at a bank can only occur after the bank is closed 9pm to 6 am
- A weekend cut over of a software package or upgrade
- Testing of a product that requires a 24/7 test
- A task that must occur on second shift
- A task applied to a resource in an alternate time zone

The first step in using task calendars is creating the calendar using the same process described in Chapter 3, *Start a Project* to create a base calendar. After the calendar is created, it then may be applied to task. There is an option to ignore the resource calendars and allow the scheduling of the resources to be directed by the task calendar for the specific task only.

To assign a calendar to a task:

1. Double-click any cell in the desired task row to launch Task Information.
2. Click the **Advanced** tab.
3. In the **Calendar** drop-down list, choose the desired calendar.
4. If desired, click **Scheduling ignores resource calendars**.
5. Click **OK**.

Figure 6-11   Advanced Tab of Task Information Dialog Box.

A visual indicator will appear in the Indicator column in the Gantt chart view.

Figure 6-12   Visual Indicator.

    Task calendars may be applied to automatically scheduled tasks or manually scheduled tasks.

Move Project

When a project's start date needs to be altered, you should determine if there are deadlines in the schedules and if those need to be taken into account. In this section, you will learn about the two techniques to move a project's start date and what to use if your schedule incorporates deadlines.

Moving the Entire Project Timeline

Typically a project start date might change between the time the project is planned and the project actually starts. There are several methods available to change the project start date. It is important that the tasks are re-scheduled to adjust to the new start date.

The easiest way to change the project start date is use the Project Information box. Changing the start date using this method will move all tasks **without entered dates or constraints** to be rescheduled as of the new start date.

To change the project start date:

1. Click the **Project** tab
2. Click **Project Information** in the Properties group
3. In the **Start date** field, enter or choose the desired new date
4. Click **OK**

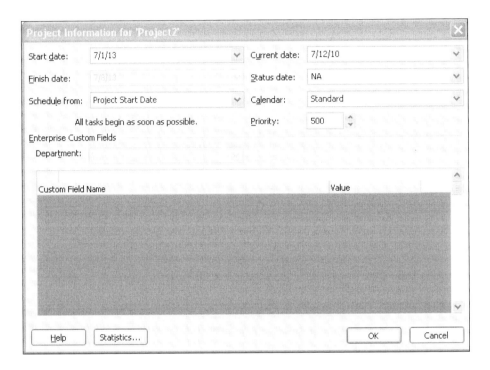

Figure 6-13   Project Information Dialog Box.

Changing the project start date will not reschedule tasks which have entered dates or constraints. Project 2013 provides a function called **Move Project** which will move all of the tasks to the new project start date. When tasks with constraints are moved using this function, the constraint dates will be adjusted based on the new project start date.

For example: if a task has a constraint 3 months from the start date of the project and the project start date is moved 6 months the constraint date will be re-scheduled 3 months from the new project start date.

The **Move Project** function also has an option to move project deadlines. If this option is not selected, the Deadlines will remain at the original dates and will need to be updated manually.

To move a project:

1. Click the **Project** tab
2. Click **Move Project** in the Schedule group

3. In the **New project start date** field, enter or choose the desired new date
4. Click **Move deadlines**
5. Click **OK**

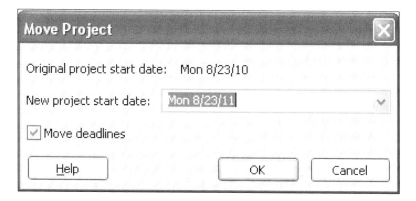

Figure 6-14   Move Project Dialog Box.

Any task that is not already linked in the schedule will move to the new start date that you enter using either of the methods above.

When you start a project as either a blank schedule or from a template, changing the project start date is recommended as a first step. If your project is fully planned out and has any type of task-related locked dates including deadlines or constraints, moving the project is recommended. This is especially useful when funding for a fully planned project has been delayed.

Task Notes

Providing comments or notes on a task could be a useful way to record business situations or explanatory details in your schedule. In this section, you will learn how experienced schedulers create notes very quickly.

Adding Notes to Tasks

Each task has a free-form notes field. The notes field may contain several types of information such as objects, hyperlinks, bulleted lists, etc. Notes may be printed on reports, exported to Excel and may be used as needed throughout the life of the project schedule.

To add a task note:

1. Method 1
    a. Double-click any cell in the desired task row to launch Task Information.
    b. Click the **Notes** tab
    c. Enter the note
    d. Click **OK**
2. Method 2
    a. Select any cell in the desired task row
    b. Click the **Task** tab
    c. Click **Task Notes** in the Properties group
    d. Enter the note
    e. Click **OK**

Figure 6-15   Notes Icon.

The notes view for a task is shown below:

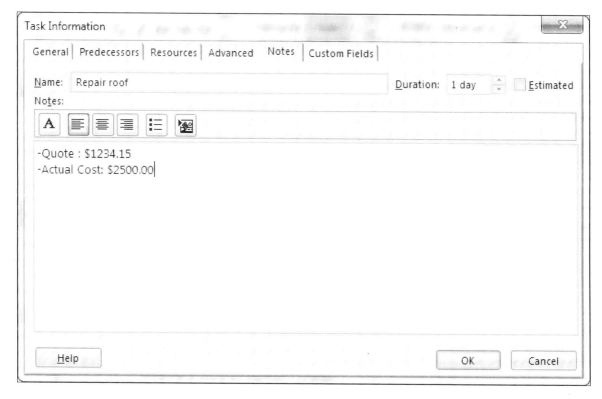

Figure 6-16   Notes Tab of Task Information Dialog Box.

The Indicator column provides a visual indicator that a task note exists. Hovering the pointer over the icon will display the note preview to give the reader an idea of its content.

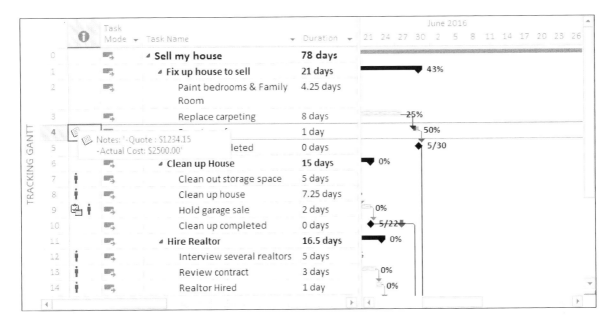

Figure 6-17   Notes Pop-Up Display.

Notes can be invaluable and should be used during the planning and execution of the project. After the project is completed and a post-project review is conducted, task note information will help in recalling details of what occurred during the performance of tasks.

Lengthy task notes might be better suited for storage in an external document that is hyperlinked to your schedule.

Key Points to Remember

- As Soon As Possible is the default constraint type for forward scheduling and is most popular.
- The constraint feature restricts Project's ability to keep a schedule dynamic and should be used sparingly.
- The deadline feature is useful to keep track of key dates or targets and provides useful indicators in your schedule.
- The Planning Wizard provides useful messages and these messages can be turned on or off as needed.
- Splitting a task divides it into sections and can be used to help accommodate working around another task.
- If you need to accommodate a unique timeframe for a task outside the standard project calendar, a task-specific calendar is a good solution.
- There are two options for moving the project timeline. Use the Move Project feature when deadlines or constraints need to be moved.
- Notes allow you to record comments on tasks.

ADVISICON®

Chapter 7
Resources

"Human communities depend upon
a diversity of talent, not a single
conception of ability. At the heart of
the challenge is to reconstitute our
sense of ability and of intelligence."
~ Sir Ken Robinson

Overview

An important first step to getting the work done that has been illustrated in the schedule is planning out the need for different types of resources that will be required. Project provides for three types of resources:

- Work
- Material
- Cost

The available quantity of each of these resources vary from project to project. Each resource type has an option to incorporate cost which can be used later on in a report. Resources are created using the Resource Sheet and its available features. After resources are fully planned out, they will be available for resource assignments.

Resource Types: Work, Material, Cost

Resources are an important part of a planned schedule. Project 2013 has the ability to offer multiple types of resources to help accomplish the work of a project. The different types of resources are intended to provide flexibility to address most types of resources required during the planning and management of a project.

We will discuss the resource types and their intended use:

1. Work resources
2. Cost resources
3. Materials resources

Work Resources

Assigning work resources to a project will allow for resource requirement forecasting and project scheduling based on resource availability. Work resources are usually human resources but can also be facilities, equipment rental and other types of resources. Work resources are given an hourly rate. Resource costs can be forecast using resource assignments to provide projected project budgets.

Effective uses of Work Resources are:

- Individual people – actual named resources
- Generic resources – these are job titles that can be used as placeholders to identify resources by skill type, skill level or if a resource is unknown. For example: DBA, Developer Level 1, Event Planner, Plumber
- Consolidated resources – used to state the quantity of a specific type of resource. For example: Helpdesk, Movers, Painters, Attendees, Members

- Facilities – a room or area that must be reserved for a period of time
- Contracted resources – external contracted labor
- Equipment – a machine that is priced by the hour

Cost Resources

Cost Resources are defined as a type of cost that occurs one or more times during the project but has a variable amount. Use of Cost resources enables the scheduler to add estimated costs during the planning phase of the project and the ability to categorize these costs. These costs will be updated into the baseline. When actual costs become available during tracking, the actual costs will be updated and compared against the original estimates to provide a variance.

Cost resources will inherently increase the cost for a task and for the project. Cost resources have no effect on work or duration. The cost amount is applied to tasks as a flat amount at the time of assigning the cost resource to a task.

Effective uses of Cost resources are:

- Travel expenses estimated in advance
- Meal expenses estimated In advance
- Expenses for something used on the project that has a varying value each time it is used, such as a permit or license renewal

Project allows for as many cost resources as needed but for simplicity try to consolidate cost resources and keep them to a limited number. The type of reporting required for the project would drive the quantity of cost resources that will be needed.

If your project includes fixed price contracts and you would like to include those on the project, you may want to consider assigning the vendor as a cost resource to a task and entering the value of the contract. If it you do not need to incorporate the vendor name, you should probably use the Fixed Cost field to record the value.

Material Resources

Material resources are defined as consumables. For example: Reference books for a new product might cost $50 each and 20 books are needed. A material resource would be created with a cost of $50 per book. An assignment would be entered for a task for 20 books. As a result $1,000 is added to the cost of the project. During tracking, the actual cost of the books purchased would be provided.

The cost of the material resources are added to the total cost of the project and updated into the project baseline. Material resources do not affect work or duration.

Effective uses of Material resources are:

- Construction: create a material resource for the cost of 1 foot of trim. Enter the number of feet required for the task
- Conference: create a material resource for the cost of giveaway bags. Enter the number of giveaway bags needed for the conference

If your project will be using a large quantity of materials such as a construction project, using Excel might be less work and a more effective means of keeping track of materials.

All resource and fixed costs are summed into the Cost field which becomes the planned budget for the project and is captured in the baseline cost.

Resource Sheet

The Resource Sheet is where all resource records are stored. Work and material resources store their costs on the resource sheet; while cost resources have a unique cost added each time they are assigned to a task.

> The quantity of a resource is determined when the resource is assigned to the task. For example, the number of hours a work resource will be needed comes from the task estimate. The number of units of a material resource is modified when the resource is assigned to the task. Normally a cost resource is always assigned at one unit on a task.

To display the Resource Sheet:

1. Click the **Task** tab
2. Click the drop-down arrow on **Gantt Chart** in the **View** group
3. Click **Resource Sheet**

The default table of the Resource Sheet is called the entry table which is shown below. This table is a subset of many of the resource fields of information that are available. This table represents the most common fields that are needed for a resource. More information is accessible through the Resource Information dialog box which will be discussed later in this chapter.

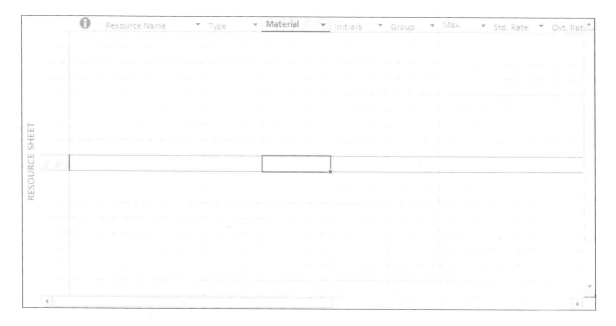

Figure 7-1   Resource Sheet View.

To enter a resource, type the resource name in the "Resource Name" field. The Resource Name is the key field for the resource data.

Project does not allow commas in the resource name field.

Many reports and assignment views will display resources in alphabetical order. A standard of last name first name allows for easy location of resources while making assignments.

After the resource name is entered, several fields will be populated with default information.

Change the resource type before entering any information to enable/disable the appropriate fields on the resource sheet.

	ⓘ	Resource Name	▼	Type	▼	Material	▼	Initials	▼	Group	▼	Max	▼	Std. Rate	▼
1		ABC Painting		Work				A				100%		$30.00/hr	

Figure 7-2   Resource Type Field in Resource Sheet View.

Descriptions of the fields on the resource sheet are provided below:

Type: Work is the default and will establish the value entered in the resource name field as a work resource. Other values are material and cost and can be changed by clicking the drop down arrow and changing the type selection.

Material: Used for Material resources only – skip for work and cost resources.

Initials: If desired, enter initials for resources. Initials may be substituted on Gantt Charts or reports as needed to shorten reports.

Group: Group is an optional field which supports the entry of numbers and text. It is usually used for department, location or skill set. This information is used to generate reports by groupings of resources.

Organizations should set a standard for the use of this field to help schedulers work with different projects more effectively.

Max units: The Max units' value is an indicator of the quantity of a resource that is available. For work resources you should enter the value for the resource on the project. The default value is 100%. When entering a group resource such as the number of people on the Helpdesk, enter the number of resources in the group. Each resource represents 1 unit. For example if there are 5 people on the Helpdesk, enter 500% in the Max Units column. For material resources, this field is unavailable since the assumption is that you can purchase more materials. For cost resources, this field is also unavailable since you manually provide a cost, no calculation is needed with units.

The default value for max units is a percentage format, but can also be displayed in a decimal format as desired.

Standard rate: Enter the desired rate for the resource that you want to have used in calculations.

Overtime rate: Enter an overtime rate for the resource. Keep in mind, it will affect only overtime hours entered.

> If your overtime rate is a value calculated against the standard rate (e.g. time and 1/2), you need to figure out the calculation and enter the grand total in the overtime rate. Project with use the overtime rate value in place of the standard rate value not in addition to.

Cost per use: An extra value that may be added to a task over and above the Standard Rate for the resource. For example: A repairman is called to fix a refrigerator. The repairman charges a transportation charge, and hourly rate, plus parts. The cost per use is the transportation charge and would be applied to every task the repairman would be assigned to.

Accrue at: Cost accrual is an indicator of a point in time when costs are incurred. Cost accrual settings have 3 options: incur costs at the start of the task, incur costs at the end of the task, or incur costs throughout the task (prorated). Prorated accrual is the default option.

Base calendar: Each work resource will have a resource calendar associated with it. The resource calendar is based on calendars that have been previously established for the project. The Standard Calendar is the default resource Base Calendar. If the base calendar contains company non-working time it is not necessary to reestablish company holidays, statutory holidays, etc. as all of these will be applied to the resources. Use the drop-down list to select the appropriate calendar for a resource.

Code: This field is available for additional information about a resource that you might want to track such as a cost center or department code.

The Resource Information dialog box is used to record information about a resource that is not captured in the Resource Sheet.

To view the Resource Information dialog box:

1. Click the **Resource** tab
2. Click **Information** in the View group

An alternate method is to right-click the resource name and click Information. You can also double-click some empty white space next to a resource name to open the same dialog box.

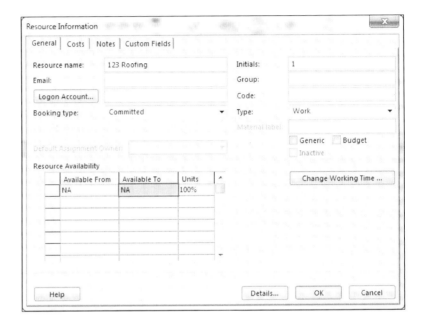

Figure 7-3   Resource Information Dialog Box.

General tab data:

Email: optional

Logon Account: optional

Booking Type, Default Assignment Owner, Inactive: Project Server only

Generic: Optional. Select this option to indicate that the resource is a generic resource. A generic resource is a skill or role type resource to be used as a holding value until a human resource is assigned. When generic resources are used, the default base calendar is used for scheduling.

Budget: An attribute applied to a resource to limit it to project-level budgeting.

This feature is discussed in our book *Advanced Scheduling with Microsoft Project: Power Scheduling from Project MVPs.*

Resource availability: Enter dates if the resource is only available for a particular period of time or has limited availability for a particular period of time. For example: An outside contractor is hired for a specific length of time. Enter the date range the resource will be available.

Calendar

Change Working Time button:

Use this option to create a specific calendar exception for a resource. This could incorporate vacation time or alternate working hours.

This dialog box is identical to the one used to change project and base calendars discussed in an earlier chapter. The calendar displayed automatically includes the settings based on the calendar you selected for the resource base calendar. This saves time since corporate exceptions are already included. Changes to this calendar are made in the same way that changes were made to the project calendar.

Click **OK** to save changes and return to the Resource Information dialog box.

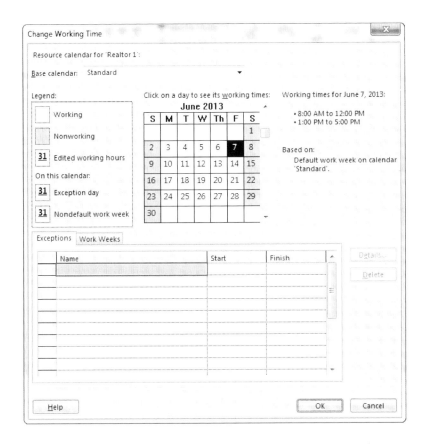

Figure 7-4   Change Working Time Dialog Box.

Cost tab data:

This tab is reserved for recording increases to costs of resources.

Most organizations who track costs experience periodic rate changes. The effective date allows early storage of future rate adjustments that become active based on a cut-off date. If a project spans the cut-off date, the tasks before the cut-off date of the project will be charged at the earlier rate and the remaining tasks which exceed the cut-off date will contain the increased rate. It is easy to see that if a project runs late, the cost of the project will increase when resource rates increase.

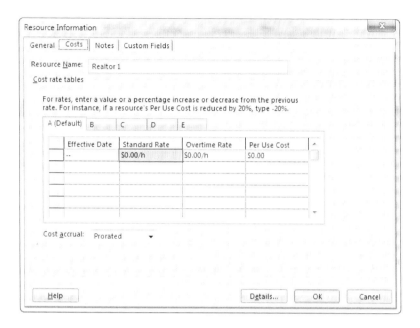

Figure 7-5   Costs Tab of the Resource Information Dialog Box.

Notes tab data:

Resource notes are treated the same as task notes within Project 2013.
Resource note data has the same formatting and flexibility as task notes.

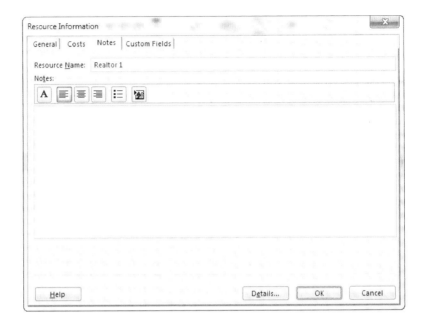

Figure 7-6   Notes Tab of the Resource Information Dialog Box.

Custom Fields tab data:

This tab is reserved for Project Server or other applications that integrate with Project.

Figure 7-7   Add Resources Menu from Add Resource Icon on
Resource Sheet View.

Material Resources

Material resources are supplies to be used by the project, such as paint, building materials, equipment, etc. Material resources are valued based on the quantity of material to be used which is assigned to a task.

Below are the fields associated with Material resources.

Resource name: name of the consumable item

Type: Material

Material label: boxes, gallons, feet, each – the label that describes the material

Standard rate: the per unit/each price

	Resource Name	Type	Material	Initials	Group	Max.	Std. Rate	Ovt. Rate	Cost/Use
1	ABC Painting	Work		A		100%	$30.00/hr	$0.00/hr	$0.00
2	Garage Sales Express	Work		G		100%	$40.00/hr	$0.00/hr	$0.00
3	XYZ Carpeting	Work		X		100%	$50.00/hr	$0.00/hr	$0.00
4	123 Roofing	Work		1		100%	$50.00/hr	$0.00/hr	$0.00
5	Realtor 1	Work		R		100%	$0.00/hr	$0.00/hr	$0.00
6	Realtor 2	Work		R		100%	$0.00/hr	$0.00/hr	$0.00
7	Realtor 3	Work		R		100%	$0.00/hr	$0.00/hr	$0.00
8	Homeowner 1	Work		H		100%	$0.00/hr	$0.00/hr	$0.00
9	Homeowner 2	Work		H		100%	$0.00/hr	$0.00/hr	$0.00
10	Helper 1	Work		H		100%	$0.00/hr	$0.00/hr	$0.00
11	Helper 2	Work		H		100%	$0.00/hr	$0.00/hr	$0.00
12	Helper 3	Work		H		100%	$0.00/hr	$0.00/hr	$0.00
13	Movers	Work		M		1,000%	$30.00/hr	$0.00/hr	$0.00
14	Moe	Work		M		100%	$0.00/hr	$0.00/hr	$0.00
15	Larry	Work		L		100%	$0.00/hr	$0.00/hr	$0.00
16	Curly	Work		C		100%	$0.00/hr	$0.00/hr	$0.00

Figure 7-8 Resource Sheet Entering Material Resources.

Cost Resource

Cost resources are used to apply estimated costs to specific tasks in a project. Estimated costs are entered during the planning stage and tracked when actual costs are entered during the execution or control stage of the project.

To enter a cost resource:

Resource name: For example: Cost travel, Cost food, Cost room rental, etc.

Type: Cost

No other information is required. The amount of the cost will be added at the time the assignment is created.

When naming cost resources include "Cost" as the first word in the name. It will be helpful when assigning cost resources as the name will give an indication of the resource type. Resources appear in alphabetical order when creating assignments and including "Cost" as the first word ensures all Cost resources will be grouped together in the list.

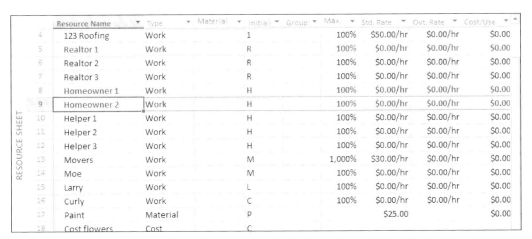

	Resource Name	Type	Material	Initial	Group	Max.	Std. Rate	Ovt. Rate	Cost/Use
4	123 Roofing	Work		1		100%	$50.00/hr	$0.00/hr	$0.00
5	Realtor 1	Work		R		100%	$0.00/hr	$0.00/hr	$0.00
6	Realtor 2	Work		R		100%	$0.00/hr	$0.00/hr	$0.00
7	Realtor 3	Work		R		100%	$0.00/hr	$0.00/hr	$0.00
8	Homeowner 1	Work		H		100%	$0.00/hr	$0.00/hr	$0.00
9	Homeowner 2	Work		H		100%	$0.00/hr	$0.00/hr	$0.00
10	Helper 1	Work		H		100%	$0.00/hr	$0.00/hr	$0.00
11	Helper 2	Work		H		100%	$0.00/hr	$0.00/hr	$0.00
12	Helper 3	Work		H		100%	$0.00/hr	$0.00/hr	$0.00
13	Movers	Work		M		1,000%	$30.00/hr	$0.00/hr	$0.00
14	Moe	Work		M		100%	$0.00/hr	$0.00/hr	$0.00
15	Larry	Work		L		100%	$0.00/hr	$0.00/hr	$0.00
16	Curly	Work		C		100%	$0.00/hr	$0.00/hr	$0.00
17	Paint	Material		P			$25.00		$0.00
18	Cost flowers	Cost		C					

Figure 7-9   Resource Sheet View Entering Cost Resources.

Key Points to Remember

- Work resources represent people.
- Material resources represent consumable items.
- Cost resources represent a general expense that varies every time it occurs.
- Use Resource Sheet view to enter the different types of resources that will be used on the project.
- Work resources have an hourly rate.
- Material resources have a price per unit.
- Cost resources only have a dollar amount when assigned to a task.
- Work resources are assigned to a calendar for the project but may have additional exception periods for vacation time or alternate working periods.

ADVISICON®

Chapter 8
Work Assignments

"Work is of two kinds: first, altering the position of matter at or near the earth's surface relatively to other such matter; second, telling other people to do so. The first kind is unpleasant and ill paid; the second is pleasant and highly paid."

~ Bertrand Russell

Overview

A schedule is merely a to-do list until you add resources to it. A resource is the person or entity who performs the work. The process of adding resources drives calculations in Project which may include the duration or work values.

Becoming familiar with task type and effort-driven settings before you assign resources will help ensure your schedule is calculated using your preferred method. There are a number of ways to assign resources which allow for single or multiple assignments at once. You can choose a variety of assignment methods based on specific task circumstances.

What is an Assignment?

The "what" of the project are the tasks which represent what work needs to be accomplished. The resources are the "who" or who will perform the work. The assignment is applying the resource to the task to create the "when" and for "how much" (cost and time). How the assignment is created will result in different outcomes for the values in the assignment. The values used in creating the assignment will drive the result for the duration, work and quantity of the resource assigned to the task. In this chapter, we will discuss techniques you can apply to generate the desired calculation result.

Review of Task Types and Effort-Driven Scheduling

Understanding task types and effort-driven settings are essential to understanding how Project performs calculations. Earlier we discussed what these terms mean and it would be helpful to review them before we create work assignments.

Effort-driven: A task set to effort driven means resources are able to work together on a task and therefore hours should be divided across the resources. Effort-driven can be turned on or off with Fixed Duration and Fixed Units tasks.

Project 2013 allows for 3 task types for scheduling:

- **Fixed Duration**: A fixed duration task is a task created with a fixed length of time.

- **Fixed Units**: Fixed Units is the quantity of resource assigned to a task and is the default task type. The quantity can be expressed in hours or a percentage of a whole resource.
- **Fixed Work**: The work of the task is fixed. Fixed work tasks are always effort-driven by default. The more resources assigned to the task, the less time the task will take to be completed because the work is divided over the resources.

When coupled with the effort-driven option, the scheduling engine allows for 5 combinations of task type, effort-driven settings:

- Fixed Duration, Effort-driven on
- Fixed Duration, Effort-driven off
- Fixed Units, Effort-driven on
- Fixed Units, Effort-driven off
- Fixed Work, Effort-driven on

To create effective resource scheduling assignments it is imperative that the task types and effect-driven settings for the tasks are correct. Different settings deliver different results during assignment creation.

> Summary tasks are always Fixed Duration and cannot be changed.

Manually scheduled tasks vs. Automatic scheduled tasks:

- The scheduling engine ignores task type and effort-driven flags for manually scheduled tasks. These values apply only to automatically scheduled tasks.

If a task is changed from manual scheduling to automatic scheduling, the task type and effort-driven values become meaningful. The value for these fields will be picked up from the options default settings when the task is entered. These values should be rechecked when switching modes to ensure correctness.

Task Type Scenarios

As discussed in *Scheduling Options* on page 79, Project is set up for planning tasks by duration. This is the reason why there are question mark icons in each duration cell: they are a reminder that you did not enter a value for that task. The question mark symbol goes away after a number is entered. Typically, new and beginning users follow this approach. If a schedule is created that will not use resources, this is also the recommended approach.

This chapter introduces you to creating resources and assigning them to tasks. With the introduction of resources, your task estimating approach becomes important because as soon as a resource is assigned the scheduling engine performs a calculation.

The following scenarios will help you ensure that your preferred approach is applied when resources are assigned.

Scenario 1: Entering a Constant Duration Value

Let's say you would like to enter a duration value that remains constant regardless of the resources that are added or subtracted.

The recommended practice is to estimate the task by entering a duration value, set the task type to Fixed Duration and then assign the resources.

This will cause total work for the task to be calculated.

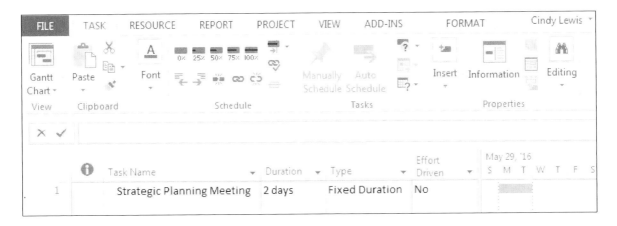

Figure 8-1   Task Entry View Formatted to Show Work Details.

The Effort Driven option provides a shortcut to divide the total work for the task across the resources assigned. This is useful for organizations that track costs or track resource assignments in detail.

To follow this approach, insert the Type and Effort Driven columns in the Entry table of Gantt Chart view or display Task Entry view which provides these fields in the lower pane. For more information about modifying views, refer to *Overview of Common Views* on page 27 and *Popular View Adjustments and Navigation* on page 35.

Scenario 2: Entering a Constant Work Value

You also have the choice to enter a total work value for the task that remains constant regardless of the resources that are added or subtracted. This is also called effort-driven estimating.

The recommended practice is to estimate the task by entering a Work value, set the task type to Fixed Work, and then assign the resources.

This will cause total duration for the task to be calculated.

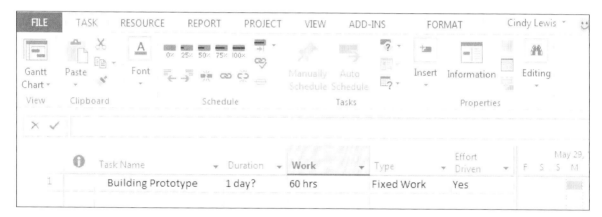

Figure 8-2　　Entry Table with Work Field.

To follow this approach, insert the Work column in the Entry table of Gantt Chart view. This is where you will enter your total Work estimate.

Do not enter anything in the Duration field. The Type field is also needed and may be inserted as a column or displayed in Task Entry view.

For more information about modifying views, refer to *Overview of Common Views* on page 27 and *Popular View Adjustments and Navigation* on page 35.

For a more detailed discussion of Task Types, refer to Chapter 3, *Advanced Work with Task Types* in our *Advanced Scheduling with Microsoft Project: Power Scheduling from Project MVPs* book.

Techniques to Assign Resources

Project provides multiple techniques to assign resources to tasks. Some methods are very quick, while other methods are more involved. Each method has advantages and disadvantages. You should decide which approach you prefer when making an assignment.

> Task Entry view or a custom Entry table with added columns are preferred when you want to see Duration, Work, Task Type, and Effort Driven fields displayed at the same time.

Assignments Using the Resource Names Column

This technique is the quickest way to make an assignment; however, additional options such as units and work for the resource are not editable.

1. Click the **Task** tab
2. Click **Gantt Chart** in the View group
3. For the desired task, click the drop-down arrow in the Resource Names column and click to assign each desired resource

Assignments Using Task Information

This technique is also a fast way to make an assignment. It is especially useful when working with cost resources so you can enter the value following the assignment.

1. Click the **Task** tab
2. Click **Gantt Chart** in the View group
3. Double-click the desired task
4. Click the Resources tab
5. On a blank row, click the drop-down arrow in the **Resource Name** column and click to assign one resource
6. Modify the values in **Units** or **Cost** if desired
7. Repeat if needed
8. Click **OK**

Assignments Using the Assign Resources Dialog Box

This technique is a good way to make an assignment when you want to assign one resource to multiple tasks or multiple resources to multiple tasks. The dialog box remains open after you complete an assignment to allow you to immediately make an additional assignment. A Units value can be manually entered in the Units field if desired when assigning a resource.

1. Click the **Task** tab
2. Click **Gantt Chart** in the View group
3. Click the **Resource** tab
4. Click **Assign Resources** in the Assignments group
5. Highlight the desired tasks, highlight the desired resources and click **Assign**
6. Modify the **Units** value if desired
7. Repeat if needed
8. Click **Close** when done

Use the Shift key to select adjacent tasks or resources. Use the Ctrl key to select non-adjacent tasks or resources.

Assignments Using Task Entry View

This technique is a good way to make an assignment when you want to focus on one task but create one or several resource assignments. It is a useful view because both the Work and Units fields are displayed and editable if desired. This option allows you to make multiple changes before you trigger the recalculation by Project. Notice the OK button is shown which indicates Project is waiting for you to finish your edits.

1. Click the **Task** tab
2. Click the drop-down arrow on **Gantt Chart** in the View group
3. Click **More Views**
4. Click **Task Entry** in the Views list
5. Click **Apply**
6. Click the desired task in the upper pane
7. On a blank row, click the drop-down arrow in the **Resource Name** column and click to assign one resource
8. Modify the values in **Units** or **Work** if desired
9. Repeat if needed
10. Click **OK**

Clicking another task or pressing the Enter key twice on the keyboard is the same as clicking the **OK** button.

Key Points to Remember

- Applying a resource to a task is an assignment.
- Task types and effort driven settings can drive schedule calculations.
- Effort driven means resources will work together on a task to accomplish it in a shorter duration.
- To plan a task with a constant duration value, choose the task type Fixed Duration.
- To plan a task with a constant work value, choose the task type Fixed Work.
- Resources can be quickly assigned using the check boxes in the Resource Names column.
- Double-click a task to assign resources with task information.
- Use the Assign Resources dialog box to do multiple task or multiple resource assignments at once.
- Task Entry view is a split screen option for assigning resources.

ADVISICON®

Chapter 9
Fine Tune the Project Schedule

"There are very few human beings
who receive the truth, complete and
staggering, by instant illumination.
Most of them acquire it fragment
by fragment, on a small scale, by
successive developments, cellu-
larly, like a laborious mosaic."

~ Anaïs Nin

Overview

Fine tuning the project schedule is about reviewing different aspects of the schedule and making the adjustments necessary to have an effective plan for going forward. During this process, you may just need to change the display of the information or you may need to make some changes that deal with resource limitations or timeline limitations. Important features of Project that help with the display include grouping, filters, and sorting which are easily implemented within columns. Identifying the critical path will help you focus your efforts on the tasks that are driving the project end date.

During your schedule evaluation, you may discover that resources are overallocated or target dates are being missed. The best way to resolve these issues is to incorporate views and analytical features to look for improvement opportunities. Some examples include Task Inspector and Team Planner view.

While Project offers the leveling feature to solve overallocations, it does have some tradeoffs against other features that can be used for resource changes. A benefit to Project is its flexibility in techniques to fine tune your project schedule and make an effective plan.

Applying Groups and Filters to Views

Most views in Project contain a table which provides a collection of columns/fields for display. These fields can be used to further refine the information displayed and potentially printed. Grouping and filtering are techniques to refine a view.

A group is a way to categorize and view information. A filter is a way to provide a subset of a collection of data. Filters hide rows of information that do not meet the condition of the filter. A highlight filter is an alternative to a regular filter and it is used to display all information, but visually shade the rows that meet the filter condition.

Groups and filters can be applied together or separately.

If you apply a built-in group or filter option, you can tailor a view even if the field(s) used is not displayed.

Filters apply to information that is currently displayed. If you have a previous filter applied or an outline level applied, your filter may not produce the desired results.

How to Apply a Group

1. Click the **View** tab
2. Click the drop-down arrow on **No Group** in the Data group
3. Click the desired group or click **More Groups**

How to Apply a Column-Based Group

1. Locate the column/field you wish to group on
2. Click the drop-down arrow on the column heading and click **Group by** to display a menu of choices
3. Click the desired option

 Click the column heading to select it and then click the drop-down arrow to generate a new choice Group on this field.

How to Remove a Group

1. Click the **View** tab
2. Click the drop-down arrow on **Group Name** in the Data group
3. Click **No Group** or **Clear Group**

How to Apply a Filter

1. Click the **View** tab
2. Click the drop-down arrow on **No Filter** in the Data group
3. Click the desired filter or click **More Filters**
4. If a dialog box appears requesting specific information, complete the information and click **OK**

How to Apply an AutoFilter

1. Locate the column/field you wish to filter on
2. Click the drop-down arrow on the column heading and select or deselect the appropriate check boxes to set the filter conditions
3. Click **OK** to apply the filter

How to Apply a Highlight Filter

1. Click the **View** tab
2. Click the drop-down arrow on **No Highlight** in the Data group
3. Click the desired filter or click **More Filters**
4. If a dialog box appears requesting specific information, complete the information and click **OK**

How to Remove All Filters

1. Click the **View** tab
2. Click the drop-down arrow on **Filter Name** in the Data group
3. Click **No Filter** or **Clear Filter**

A fast way to remove all filters is to press F3.

Built-in Groups

Groups are used to categorize information. To save time when grouping, a number of pre-configured groups are installed automatically. Gantt Chart views and other task views provide these pre-configured task groups. They are itemized in *Table 9.1.*

Table 9.1   Task Groups Provided by Default

Group name	Fields/Columns using in the Group
Active vs. Inactive	Active
Auto scheduled vs. Manually scheduled	Task Mode
Complete vs. Incomplete	% Complete
Constraint Type	Constraint Type
Critical	Critical
Duration	Duration
Duration then Priority	Duration, Priority
Milestone	Milestone
Priority	Priority
Priority keeping outline structure	Project, Outline number, Priority
Resource	Resource Name
Status	Status

Resource views provide pre-configured resource groups. They are listed in *Table 9.2*.

Table 9.2   Resource Groups Provided by Default

Group name	Fields/columns used in the group
Complete and Incomplete Resources	% Work Complete
Resource Group	Group
Resource Type	Type
Standard Rate	Standard Rate
Work vs. Material	Type

When an assignment view is displayed, assignment groups are available. *Table 9.3* illustrates an additional grouping that is available in an assignment view.

Table 9.3   Assignment Groups Provided by Default

Group Name	Fields/columns used in the group	Comments
Assignments keeping outline structure	Name, Task outline number	May only be used from Resource Usage view

Built-in Filters

Filters are used to display specified information. To save time when filtering, a number of pre-configured filters are installed automatically. Gantt Chart views and other task views provide these pre-configured task filters. They are itemized in *Table 9.4*.

Table 9.4   Task Filters Provided by Default

Filter	Fields/Columns used in the Filter	Generates a Dialog Box for Input
Active Tasks	Active	
Automatic scheduled tasks	Task Mode	
Completed Tasks	% Complete	
Costs Greater Than...	Cost	X
Cost Overbudget	Cost v Baseline cost	
Created After...	Created	X
Critical	Critical	
Date Range...	Start, Finish	X
In Progress Tasks	Actual start, Actual finish	
Incomplete tasks	% Complete, % work complete for the assignment	

Table 9.4   Task Filters Provided by Default

Filter	Fields/Columns used in the Filter	Generates a Dialog Box for Input
Late tasks	Status	
Late/Overbudget Tasks Assigned To...	Resource Name, baseline finish, Finish v Baseline finish, Cost v Baseline cost	X
Linked fields	Linked fields	
Manually Scheduled Tasks	Task Mode	
Milestones	Milestone	
Resource Groups...	Resource Groups	X
Should Start By...	Start v Actual Start	X
Slipped/ Late Tasks	Baseline Finish, Finish v baseline finish, BCWS v BCWP	
Slipping Tasks	Actual finish, Baseline finish, Finish v Baseline finish	
Summary tasks	Summary	

Table 9.4   Task Filters Provided by Default

Filter	Fields/Columns used in the Filter	Generates a Dialog Box for Input
Task range...	ID (range of task ID numbers)	X
Tasks with a Task Calendar Assigned	Task Calendar	
Tasks with Attachments	Objects, Notes	
Tasks with Deadlines	Deadline	
Tasks with estimated Durations	Estimated	
Tasks with Fixed Dates	Constraint type, actual start	
Tasks without Dates	Start, Finish	
Tasks/Assignments with Overtime	Overtime Work	
Top level tasks	Outline level	
Unstarted tasks	Actual Start	
Using Resource In Date Range...	Resource name, Start, Finish	X
Using Resource...	Resource Name	X

Table 9.4 Task Filters Provided by Default

Filter	Fields/Columns used in the Filter	Generates a Dialog Box for Input
Work overbudget	Actual Work vs. Baseline Work	

Resource views provide pre-configured resource filters. They are listed in *Table 9.5*.

Table 9.5 Resource Filters Provided by Default

Filter	Fields/Columns used in the Filter	Generates a Dialog Box for Input
Budget Resources	Budget	
Costs Greater Than...	Cost	X
Cost Overbudget	Cost v Baseline cost	
Created After...	Created	X
Date Range...	Start, Finish	X
Group...	Group	X
In Progress Assignments	Actual start, Actual finish	
Linked Fields	Linked fields	

Table 9.5   Resource Filters Provided by Default

Filter	Fields/Columns used in the Filter	Generates a Dialog Box for Input
Non-budget Resources	Budget	
Overallocated Resources	Overallocated, Assignment	
Resource Range...	ID	X
Resource - Cost...	Type	X
Resource - Material	Type	
Resource - Work	Type	
Resources With Attachments	Objects, Notes	
Resource/ Assignments With Overtime	Overtime Work	
Should Start By...	Assignments, Actual Start	X
Should Start/Finish by...	Start, Finish	X
Slipped/Late Progress	Baseline finish, Finish, BCWS	

Table 9.5   Resource Filters Provided by Default

Filter	Fields/Columns used in the Filter	Generates a Dialog Box for Input
Slipping Assignments	Actual finish, Baseline finish, Finish	
Unstarted Assignments	Actual start	
Work Complete	% Complete	
Work Incomplete	% Complete, Work	
Work Overbudget	Work v Baseline Work	

Sorting Tasks or Resources in a View

Project initially arranges tasks according to ID number which is located in the far left column of the Gantt Chart view. To make it easier to work with your tasks, you may want to temporarily or permanently rearrange them. You can rearrange the order of tasks based on a particular type of information, including start date, finish date, priority, cost, and ID.

When you sort a project that contains summary tasks, Project maintains the outline levels and bases the sort on the summary task values. For example, if you sort a group of summary tasks by start date, Project bases the order on the start date of each summary task. Project then sorts the tasks within each summary task.

You can also sort resources in most resource views. By default, resources are arranged in ascending order based on the ID number, but you can sort resources by cost or name.

You can also perform a custom sort by specifying up to three sort fields. Sorting by more than one field is helpful when more than one task contains the same information in some fields. For example, if you sort by the duration and more than one task has the same duration, you can determine the order of those tasks by sorting by an additional field, such as the start date.

To sort information within a view:

1. Click the **View** tab
2. Click the drop-down arrow on **Sort** in the Data group
3. Click the desired option or click **Sort By** for more options

How to Sort Information

1. Click the **View** tab
2. Click the drop-down arrow on **Sort** in the Data group
3. Click the desired sort option or click **Sort by**

Choosing Permanently renumber tasks in the Sort By dialog box will renumber all rows in the view. This option is not recommended in a task view, such as Gantt Chart , since that will permanently change the order of items in your schedule.

How to Apply a Column Based Sort

1. Locate the column/field you wish to sort on
2. Click the drop-down arrow on the column heading and select **Sort A to Z** or **Sort Z to A**

How to Reset a Sort Back to Default

1. Click the **View** tab
2. Click the drop-down arrow on **Sort** in the Data group
3. Click **by ID**

Critical Path

An extremely important concept in scheduling is the critical path. This should drive business decisions in your schedule. In this section you will learn more about the definition of this concept and how to use it when making decisions such as the need to apply more resources to your schedule.

What is a Critical Path

The Critical Path is the longest path of tasks through the network of tasks for the schedule. It represents the timeline of the schedule and establishes the end date for the project. It is the minimum time that it will take to complete the project. Tasks not included in the network of tasks will not be included in critical path calculation.

> For a more accurate critical path calculation, all tasks should have a predecessor and a successor except the first and last tasks of a project.

Checking the contents of the predecessor and successor columns to make sure all tasks have valid entries is helpful.

Any task on the critical path is known as a Critical Task. If a critical task slips, the end date of the project will be negatively affected.

Scheduling factors contributing to the Critical Path calculation include:

- Relationships between tasks
- Lead and Lag time

- Duration of tasks
- Constraints
- Task Calendars
- Resource Availability
- Resource Assignments

Project will automatically recalculate the critical path each time a task is changed. The calculation is making a forward and backward pass through the schedule looking for time gaps between tasks. This time gap is called slack which is also known as float. If a task has slack, it is considered non-critical. When a task has no slack, it is considered critical. Slack can be either a positive or negative value.

Every project schedule should include float or slack in order to address contingencies. No project will run exactly as planned. Float or slack will provide the extra time needed to handle unknown problems that will arise during the execution of a project.

There are 2 types of slack calculated in Project 2013:

- Total slack is the amount of time a task can slip without affecting the end date of the project.
- Free slack is the amount of time a task can slip before it affects its immediate successor task. If a task only has one successor, free slack will be the same as total slack.

This type of critical path calculation is based on tasks.

Resources can also be critical within a project schedule. During the execution of the project, different resources will become critical at different points within the schedule. If a critical resource is not available at a critical point, the entire project could be affected as well as the ending date.

Frequently, during the execution of a project, a task that was not originally on the critical path will become critical. Careful tracking and monitoring of the critical path during the management of the project will help keep the project manager on track to achieve the goal of the projected end date.

Formatting Views to Display Critical Path

Slack is essentially scheduling breathing space for a project and occurs when a particular task can be delayed without affecting the end of the project. The greater the slack, the more breathing space you will have to help manage problems that may occur during the performance of the project. If a schedule fails to include slack, the plan for the schedule might be unobtainable. Since projects are typically never performed exactly as scheduled, slack becomes essential to achieving the goal date for the project.

Each time a task is changed in Project, the critical path is recalculated automatically.

Project provides the ability to format the Gantt Chart view to identify critical tasks and tasks with slack time.

To turn on Critical Tasks and Slack formatting:

1. Click the **Format** tab
2. Click **Critical Tasks** and click **Slack** as desired in the Bar Styles group

Figure 9-1   Critical Tasks Check Box.

The critical path is shown as red Gantt bars and the non-critical tasks appear a blue Gantt bars. Once you have displayed the critical path, you will have a better understanding of the specific tasks which are driving the ending date of your project schedule.

Viewing Resource Assignments

Once assignments are created, refining them and looking at them from different points of view is not only helpful but necessary. If resource allocations and future resource demands are your goals for using Project, taking a deeper look at the results of how the assignments were created will be essential.

Resource Usage View

The purpose of the Resource Usage view is to allow viewing and updating of assignments from the resource point of view. This view displays all assignments created for a resource as well as assignment details. Information may be viewed at any level of timescale detail that is appropriate for your project.

You will be able to use this view to answer the following questions:

- How much availability does a resource have?
- What is the cost of having a resource work on a task?
- Are all of the tasks assigned to a resource?
- How many hours is a resource assigned to a task?
- Is a resource overallocated? (Overbooked)
- What is the future demand for a resource for this project?
- What is the total number of hours for a resource assigned to the project?

The Resource Usage view may be used for resource work distribution worksheets. When this view is printed, a timeframe may be added to allow for more focused printing. Insert a page break between resources to print separate reports for each resource.

Task Usage View

Task Usage view is very similar to the Resource Usage view, however, the content is shown from the task perspective. Each task is displayed with the resources assigned to the task. The scheduler will be able to see a complete picture of the details of assignments. This view may also be used for changing or fine tuning assignments. Information may be viewed at any level of timescale detail that is appropriate for your project.

- What resources are assigned to a task?
- Which tasks do not have a resource assigned?
- What is the total cost and number of hours of a task?
- What is the remaining work of a task?
- What percent allocations are my resources assigned to tasks?
- What is the distribution of work for all the resources on the task?

How to Display Resource Usage View

1. Click the **View** tab
2. Click **Resource Usage** in the Resource Views group

How to Display Task Usage View

1. Click the **View** tab
2. Click **Task Usage** in the Tasks Views group

How to Adjust Information in the TimePhased Grid on Resource Usage or Task Usage View

1. Click the **Format** tab
2. Click **Add Details** in the Details group
3. Select the desired field(s) on the left and click **Show** or select the desired field(s) on the right and click **Hide**
4. Click **OK** to apply the changes

Team Planner View

The purpose of this view is to show resources and their assignments using a Gantt style format. The team planner view will help the scheduler identify overallocations within the schedule, level workloads, reassign resources to tasks and identify problems in the schedule from the resource point of view.

Team Planner view is only available in Project 2013 Professional.

Team Planner view is divided into 2 sections. The upper section contains one row for each resource, with bars to the right representing assigned work. The lower section contains bars representing tasks without resources.

How to Display Team Planner View

1. Click the **View** tab
2. Click **Team Planner** in the Resource Views group

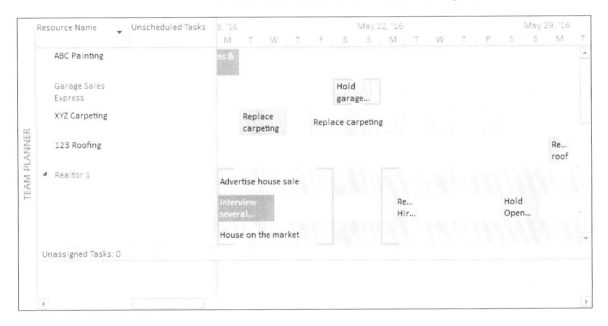

Figure 9-2   Team Planner View.

Table 9.6 will help with understanding how to interpret the information in the view:

Table 9.6   Team Planner View Legend

Feature	Description
A vertical orange line	Today's date
Tasks colored in darker blue	Progress on the task

Table 9.6   Team Planner View Legend

Feature	Description
Teal colored tasks	Manually scheduled tasks
Gray colored tasks	External tasks
Light blue colored tasks	Un-started tasks
Gaps in timelines for resources	Under-allocated resource or unavailable
Red lines on the top and bottom of the task	Overallocated tasks
Resource name in red	Overallocated resource
Task bars colored black	Tasks that are late
Shaded day on calendar	Non-working day for the resource. This data is coming from the resource availability calendar
Top pane – pink blocks of time	Overallocated time

Table 9.7 includes some of the mouse shortcuts that will help you work with the information in this view.

Table 9.7   Mouse Shortcuts for Team Planner View

Action	Result
Double click the resource name	Resource Information dialog box
Double click a work task bar	Task Information dialog box
Timescale density	Adjust as needed – lower right corner
Hover over task	Pop up of task details
Double click on timescale	Opens the timescale box to alter scale values
Right click on a task	More options:
Right click on an assignment – Reassign to:	This option presents a list of all resources in the schedule, including resources already assigned to the task. Select a resource to reassign to the task or select unassigned option and all assignments will be removed from the task.
Right click on an assignment – Inactivate:	Task will disappear from the Team Planner view. To reactive, return to Gantt chart view.

Only active tasks will show in the team planner view.

Understanding Overallocations

Each resource is assigned a calendar when entered on the Resource Sheet. The calendar is customized to contain the availability of the resource. When more work is assigned to a resource than time available on their resource calendar, the resource is considered to be overallocated. The overallocation calculation is looking at resource assignments on a minute by minute basis. If a resource is overbooked for even 1 minute, the resource is considered overallocated.

When a resource is overallocated, a red person symbol appears in the indicator column. This indicates that there is an overallocated resource assigned to the task but will not indicate which resource is affected. Even though resources are overallocated, assignments can continue to be created.

		Task Mode	Task Name	Duration	Work	Start	Finish	Prec
3			Replace carpeting	8 days	40 hrs	Tue 5/17/16	Fri 5/27/16	2
4			Repair roof	1 day	24 hrs	Mon 5/30/16	Mon 5/30/16	3
5			Fix up completed	0 days	0 hrs	Mon 5/30/16	Mon 5/30/16	4
6			⊿ **Clean up House**	**15 days**	**400 hrs**	**Mon 5/2/16**	**Sun 5/22/16**	
7			Clean out storage space	5 days	120 hrs	Mon 5/2/16	Fri 5/6/16	
8			Clean up house	7.25 days	232 hrs	Mon 5/9/16	Wed 5/18/16	7
9			Hold garage sale	2 days	48 hrs	Sat 5/21/16	Sun 5/22/16	8
10			Clean up completed	0 days	0 hrs	Sun 5/22/16	Sun 5/22/16	9
11			⊿ **Hire Realtor**	**16.5 days**	**256 hrs**	**Mon 5/2/16**	**Tue 5/24/16**	
12			Interview several realtors	5 days	200 hrs	Mon 5/2/16	Wed 5/18/16	
13			Review contract	3 days	48 hrs	Wed 5/18/16	Mon 5/23/16	12
14			Realtor Hired	1 day	8 hrs	Mon 5/23/16	Tue 5/24/16	13
15			Realtor Hired Completed	0 days	0 hrs	Tue 5/24/16	Tue 5/24/16	14
16			House ready to sell	0 days	0 hrs	Mon 5/30/16	Mon 5/30/16	15,1
17			⊿ **Selling of the house**	**60 days**	**1,776 hrs**	**Mon 5/9/16**	**Fri 7/29/16**	

Figure 9-3   Overallocated Resource Indicators in Gantt Chart View.

Real World Application of Scheduling: Shortening the Schedule and Resolving Resource Conflicts

Scheduling involves not only creating a detailed schedule and assigning resources, but it involves modifying the schedule to meet goals and to work with limitations. Typically there is a goal to complete the schedule on time and a common limitation is availability of resources. This section will address those areas.

Shortening the Schedule

Once you create your schedule, arrange the tasks, and assign resources to the tasks, you may realize that the schedule does not meet your original goals. You may have a deadline or a budget that you must meet. Listed below are several ways to shorten your schedule. The method you choose depends on your individual project and resources.

The best way to shorten your project is to shorten the critical path. The critical path includes those tasks that affect the duration of the project. If a critical task finishes late, it delays the entire project. If a critical task finishes early, it shortens the duration of the project. If you shorten the length of the critical path, you shorten the duration of your project, and your project finishes sooner.

Some options to consider for shortening the project schedule are:

- Assign additional resources
- Assign a resource to work overtime
- Increase working time (calendar)

- Break task into smaller tasks
- Overlap key activities (multi-tasking)
- Delete tasks
- Redefine quality (less time on activities)
- Break project into phases
- Change dependencies of tasks

Resolving Resource Conflicts

The most common resource conflict is that a resource is overallocated. This means they have more work assigned to them then they can realistically complete in the given time frame.

While there are multiple ways to manage resource allocation, it is important to find and analyze resource overallocation and evaluate the overall effect on the project schedule.

Some options to consider for solving resource conflicts are:

- Hire additional resources
- Replace a resource on a task
- Assign a resource to work overtime
- Increase work time (calendar)
- Break a task up and move a portion of a task till a resource is available
- Delay the entire task until a resource is available
- Adjust the division of work across the task (work contour)
- Move or create a constraint on the task until the resource is available
- Delete tasks
- Change overlapping tasks into sequential tasks
- Use Project's leveling feature
- Use Task Inspector to solve the problem
- Use Team Planner to solve the problem

Notice the similarity with features already mentioned to shorten the schedule.

Views to Identify Overallocations

There are several views in Project that will help analyze resource overallocations. After an overallocation situation is discovered, research should be carried out to understand where the overallocation exists.

The views below will help locate these problems:

- Gantt Chart view
- Resource Sheet
- Resource Graph
- Resource Allocation view
- Team Planner
- Task Usage view
- Resource Usage view

Techniques to help work with overallocations will be illustrated next. You may have already discovered some of these on your own while using Project.

Using Indicators

In the Gantt Chart view, you will immediately be notified if there is an overallocated resource on a task when the red stick figure appears. If you hover the cursor on this icon, the display indicates resources are overallocated. This indicator is a handy and quick visual cue to identify overallocated resources.

Figure 9-4   Overallocated Resource.

Using the Resource Allocation View

The Resource Allocation view is a combination view that shows resource assignments in a Resource Usage pane along with a personal Gantt chart in the lower pane. The advantage of this view is you can see both numerically and visually what a resource is working on and use either the upper or lower pane to quickly make modifications. The Resource Allocation view is useful for identifying resource commitment issues.

How to Display Resource Allocation View

1. Click the **View** tab
2. Click the drop down arrow on **Other Views** in the Resource Views group
3. Click **More Views**
4. Click **Resource Allocation**
5. Click **Apply**

Methods for Resolving Resource Conflicts

In this section, you will be exposed to many different methods for analyzing and resolving resource conflicts. It will be up to you to determine the correct mix of options for the schedule. Some methods will be more manually driven, while other methods will take advantage of some automatic features in Project. Methods that are more automated may have more of a ripple effect that aren't expected so be sure to carefully choose the appropriate method. This list of methods is not meant to cover every possible scenario, but instead is presented to give suggested scenarios that are popular and easy to use. No order of priority is indicated with this list.

Using Indicator Suggestions

For tasks that have a red stick figure in the indicators column, that means there is a resource conflict on the task. You can use shortcuts in Project to help fix that. Simply right click on the indicator field or name of the task and apply one of the options listed such as: Fix in Task Inspector or Reschedule to Available Date.

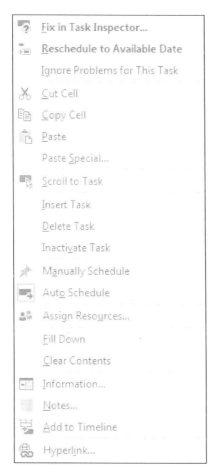

Figure 9-5   Context Menu from Overallocated Resource.

Using Task Inspector

Another option to evaluate and solve problems with the schedule is Task Inspector. Using this option gives you a pane to the left side of the Entry table. The advantage of Task Inspector is it provides critical information about the task and information about what is occurring at a specific time and gives you options to correct any issues, including hyperlinks to the feature or area where you can make a change.

How to Apply Task Inspector

1. Click the **Task** tab
2. Click **Inspect** in the Tasks group

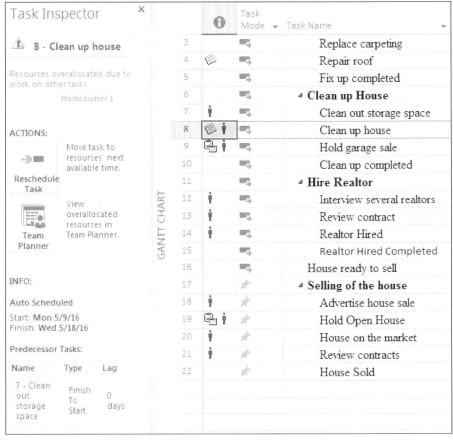

Figure 9-6   Task Inspector.

Don't forget to consider the ripple effect of making a change to one task. As other tasks respond to this change, you may see a change in the critical path or introduce other resource conflicts.

Changing Resource Assignments

When you look at resource assignments individually, you might see that one resource is very overworked; however, when you look at resources collectively, you might notice that some resources are under-worked. One of the best ways to solve resource issues is to more equitably distribute the work. For example, Ricardo is assigned to a task at 150% while Angelica is assigned to a task at the exact same time at 25%. If you can find a way to shift some of Ricardo's work to Angelica, you will take better advantage of the availability of both resources. Changing assignments can be done in many different views such as Task Usage or Resource Usage view.

When you return to the Resource Allocation view, it will recalculate and remove that task from the resource you had selected. You may need to reselect that resource again if you want to see an updated lower pane and be able to continue making adjustments.

Move a Task Until a Resource is Available

Sometimes the resource assigned to a task is the only person with the skill set that can do the work. In this case the only option is to move the task until the resource is available. One technique for moving a task is to shift by a time period (e.g. week); another technique is to reschedule the task until the resource is available.

Moving a task will create a constraint on the task.

How to Move Tasks to Account for Resource Limitations

1. Select the desired task (click on the row ID number or task name)
2. Click the **Task** tab
3. Click the drop down arrow on **Move** in the Tasks group
4. Click the desired option

Assigning a Work Contour

When you assign a resource to a task, Project spreads the work out evenly over the duration of the task unless you specify otherwise. For example, if you assign a resource 100% to work 80 hours on a ten day task, Project assigns eight hours of work per day. This is a flat contour.

Not all tasks require that the work be spread equally (a flat contour). For example, consider the building of a fine custom wooden cabinet, which is one task in a project that involves furnishing a house. The carpenter purchases the wood and other components, which requires trips to several specialty stores. He spreads the trip out over several days, while using some of his time to finish his previous project. Then he works full days for three weeks cutting and assembling the cabinet. In the middle of construction, he puts in some overtime.

After the construction phase is completed, he stains the wood, which takes two hours. The stain has to dry overnight. The next day, he applies a coat of varnish, which takes two hours. It, too, has to dry overnight.

The next day, he sands the varnish and applies another coat, which takes three hours. He applies three more coats of varnish, repeating the progress.

On the last day, he buffs the final coat, which takes an hour. Most of the work on the cabinet occurs during the middle of the project, peaking during a few days of overtime. Work at the beginning and end of the task is part-time.

You can change the work contour by manually modify the working hours in the time-phased grid on the right side of the Task Usage or Resource Usage views.

Using the Team Planner View

The Team Planner view is very visually pleasing and allows you to manage your schedule by resources instead of by task. Overallocations can be quickly corrected here and the impact on the resource or other resources is immediately visible.

The Team Planner view is an interactive format allowing you to drag and drop activities directly on the right portion of the screen to alleviate overallocations.

To use the Team Planner View to solve an overallocation:

- Locate the task that is causing a conflict (red lines above/below highlight the task), and simply drag the task to a new time period for the same resource or drag it to another resource.

    Optionally – You can right click on the task and take advantage of features available in the short-cut menu (such as reassign to another resource).

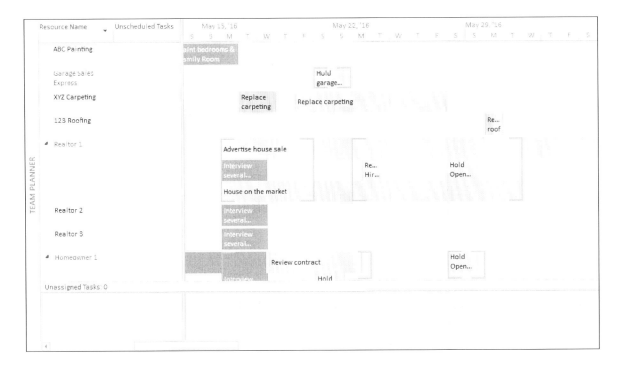

Figure 9-7   Team Planner View.

The Team Planner view is also an easy way to assign tasks that currently do not have resources assigned to them. Unassigned tasks will appear at the bottom of the Team Planner view and can be dragged and dropped to the appropriate resource.

Dragging a task to a new location will create a constraint on that task since you are essentially forcing it to happen a particular time. If you want to avoid constraints, use the Gantt Chart view and make other adjustments such as changing links or reassigning tasks.

Applying Leveling Features

Leveling is a feature in Project that can be used to solve overallocations. While the software can't dream up a creative solution, it is able to shift, delay, and split tasks to take advantage of open spaces in your project where resources might be underallocated or where tasks can be delayed without shifting the end date. Should you choose, you can also indicate that your end date is flexible so there are more options for leveling to correct overallocations. Before you use leveling, be sure to consider the following scenarios and options.

These are three leveling scenarios you can choose:

Level Selection – use this option when you are in a task view and want to fix overallocated resources on specific tasks. This will leave overallocations for those same resources on other tasks untouched. Typically this option can help when you need to make sure you meet your commitments on the selected task(s), but do not want to address other tasks at the same time.

Level Resource – use this option when you are in a resource view and want to fix overallocations by resource. This choice would be suggested when you know that the availability of a specific resource will not change and you have to get the work done using this limited availability.

Level All – this option is when you want to fix overallocations across the entire project across all resources.

When you click Leveling Options, the following dialog box appears:

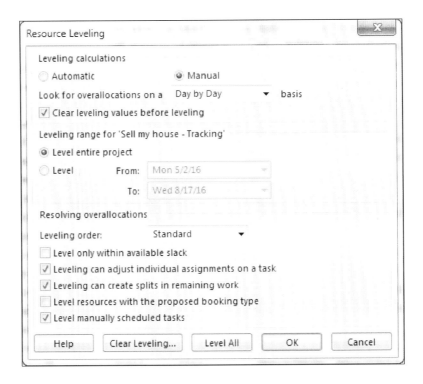

Figure 9-8   Resource Leveling Diagram.

Please consider the following when selecting your options:

- Automatic is not recommended since it will level your project continuously without warning. Tasks will be delayed before you realize anything has happened.
- While Project offers an auto leveling feature to resolve overallocation, it is recommended that the project manager resolve overallocation manually. Overallocation can be a complex issue and requires analysis. Utilizing the auto leveling feature can diminish your ability to analyze and uncover the root cause of the overallocation.
- Consider changing Leveling order to "Priority, Standard" if you have set priority numbers on your tasks.
- Best Practice – Only use priority numbers to lock exception tasks down. For example, setting a task to a priority number of 1000 will make sure that they task does not move when you level. Essentially you are setting the task to be highest priority.

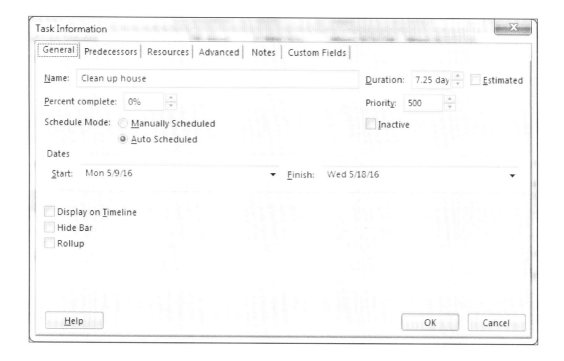

Figure 9-9   Task Information Dialog – General Tab.

- "Level only within available slack" attempts to delay only non-critical tasks. The drawback to this feature is it limits Project's ability to fix things.
- Best Practice – Run leveling first with the "Level only within available slack" option enabled to protect your critical path and observe the benefits before turning this option off and running unrestricted leveling.
- "Leveling can adjust individual assignments on a task" means when a task is staffed with multiple resources, Project has the flexibility to move work resource by resource instead of moving the entire task and all resources at once.
- "Leveling can create splits in remaining work" means a task can be split as needed to get around other tasks that can't be moved.

Be sure to review the splits created in your Project and undo the action if necessary. For example, if the result of this is a task that is split into 10 pieces, this is probably not a good result.

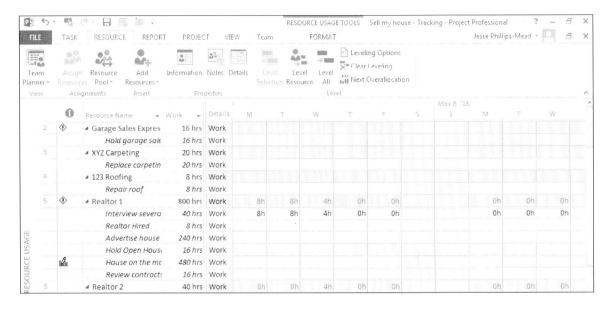

Figure 9-10   Leveling.

How to Apply Resource Leveling

1. Click the **Resource** tab
2. Click Leveling Options in the Level group
3. Choose desired options and click **OK** to save the settings or click **Level Now** to apply resource leveling immediately

> To level by a specific resource, click **OK** on the leveling options and click Level Resource to choose a specific resource.

How to Clear Resource Leveling

1. Click the **Resource** tab
2. Click **Clear Leveling** in the Level group

Key Points to Remember

- Use a group to categorize information in a view.
- Use a filter to identify a subset of information meeting a specific criteria in a view.
- Views are sorted by ID number by default but can be resorted as desired.
- The Critical Path is the longest path of tasks through the network of tasks for the schedule.
- The Format tab has a shortcut checkbox to display the critical path.
- Views for analyzing assignments include Task Usage view, Resource Usage view and Team Planner view.
- Shortening the schedule means shortening the critical path.
- Options to shorten the critical path are applied manually by the scheduler.
- In Resource Sheet view, Resource Usage View, and Resource Allocation view an overallocated resource is displayed in red and bold.
- A red overallocation indicator appears in Gantt Chart view in the Indicators column when a resource is overallocated on a specific task.
- There are numerous methods to resolve resource conflicts, the majority of which are applied manually by the scheduler.
- Task inspector provides an analysis of the factors that are impacting the task and offers suggestions.
- Replacing a resource on a task is a great way to solve an overallocation – especially if a resource is underutilized.
- Tasks can be individually moved until a resource is available to solve an overallocation but it will create a task constraint.
- Varying the daily hours a resource is working on a task is contouring and can help balance work across multiple tasks on the same day.
- Use Team Planner view to visually analyze the schedule by resource.
- Team Planner view has a convenient click and drag option to move conflicting tasks to another time period or another resource.
- Leveling can shift, delay or split tasks to solve resource overallocations.
- Level Now is what you click to level the schedule, not OK.
- Turn on the "Level only within available slack" option initially when leveling to evaluate the least impact to the schedule.

ADVISICON®

Chapter 10
Baseline and Tracking

"To doubt everything or to believe
everything are two equally convenient solutions; both dispense
with the necessity of reflection."

~ Henri Poincaré

Overview

After a schedule is refined and approved, you are ready to begin the work of the project. Often stakeholders will request the ability to see status updates throughout the project and how the delivery of the project tasks vary from the original plan. In order to illustrate variances from the original schedule, you will need to set a baseline. A baseline is a way to capture fields that are needed for variance views and variance calculations.

Tracking of the project involves updating the completion status of tasks and may involve entering values that differ from the original task (such as a delayed start date). After tasks are tracked, you can use Tracking Gantt view to see how those tasks performed against their baseline values.

The Importance of Baselining

One of the integral parts of the decision making process is being aware of where the schedule stands against its original plan. The baseline is the original plan.

After the schedule has been adjusted, discussed and negotiated with the stakeholders of the project, a schedule will be agreed upon. That original approved schedule will be set as the project baseline. The project baseline becomes the schedule that the metrics for the project will measure against. It is also the plan that the stakeholders are expecting the project performers to adhere to during the project.

When an event occurs to put the project off schedule, the difference between the actual performance values and the baseline values is known as the variance. Variances can have either a positive or negative effect on the schedule. Monitoring variances gives the project manager more knowledge regarding the project which in turn results in better decision making to adjust the project schedule if needed or help the project get back on track.

Without a baseline, this knowledge would be lost. You would not be aware of how off track the schedule is from the original planned finish date and you would not have a finish date to manage the schedule against.

> Project requires a baseline to calculate earned value. More information about this topic is in the *Advanced Scheduling with Microsoft Project: Power Scheduling from Project MVPs* where we cover *Costing, Budgets and Earned Value*.

Setting a Baseline

A critical component before you begin tracking is to set the baseline. After your project is formally approved and right before work is ready to begin, setting a baseline will capture information about what you have planned so you can use it as a measure against how the project actually performs. Because it is available for comparison purposes at any point during the project, the baseline provides an effective way to check your progress throughout the project. Project deals with three levels of time when working with projects: baseline, current, and actual.

> You should not set the baseline until you are finished entering tasks and creating the schedule. The goal is to have the schedule as complete as possible before setting a baseline for comparison purposes.

The act of setting a baseline creates a copy of the following fields into equivalent baseline fields (e.g., Baseline Start):

- Start
- Finish
- Duration
- Work
- Cost

Baseline information is always maintained unless you set a subsequent baseline again for the entire project. In many cases you will not need to use Baseline 1–10, but very lengthy projects may want to use the additional baselines to capture a snapshot at the end of each year (as an example).

To set the baseline:

1. Click the **Project** tab.
2. Click the drop-down arrow on **Set Baseline** in the Schedule group.
3. Click **Set Baseline**.
4. Click **OK**.

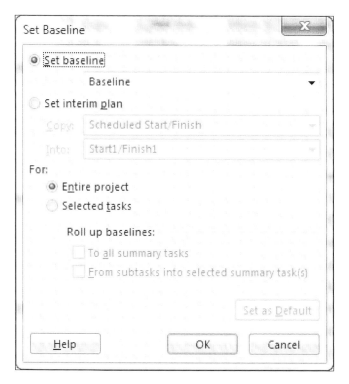

Figure 10-1   Set Baseline Dialog Box – Setting Baseline.

To utilize the variance calculations, you must record the current baseline using the first option from the drop-down menu listed as just "Baseline." Project calculates from this Baseline only. This Baseline is also known as Baseline 0. Baselines 1–10 are for historical purposes only, but you may use any numbered baseline in a view.

As a best practice, create a backup copy of your original baseline data by immediately setting the baseline again and using an empty baseline 1–10. This way even if you accidentally overwrite the information in the first Baseline, you can still retrieve it by going to your backup baseline. This also provides historical information about previous baselines.

Setting an Interim Plan

Setting an interim plan follows the same procedures as setting the baseline except that you chose **Interim** as the option. The main purpose for the interim plan is to capture historical snap-shots of the current state of a project at specific points in time. Use this feature instead of making duplicate copies of your schedule. Another alternative use for this feature to extend the number of baselines available to the project manager.

Clearing a Baseline

While it is best practice to maintain copies of baselines for historical purposes, it may be necessary to clear a baseline. For example, a baseline set by mistake.

To clear a baseline:

1. Click the **Project** Tab.
2. Click the drop-down arrow on **Set Baseline** in the Schedule group.
3. Click **Clear Baseline**.
4. If necessary, click the drop-down arrow to the right of **Clear baseline plan** to change the baseline that will be cleared.
5. Click **OK**.

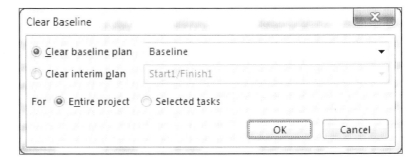

Figure 10-2   Clear Baseline Dialog Box.

Updating Baseline

When approved changes are made to the schedule, the changes might result in a change to the baseline. Each organization should have a policy in place as to when or how baselines should be updated. Baselines, at times, are misunderstood by project schedulers and organizations should clarify their policies and intended usage. Management may want to be alerted when baselines have been updated or overwritten.

Baseline updates may include selected tasks, overwriting the existing Baseline 0, or capturing a new baseline in Baseline 1-10 fields.

> Project views such as Tracking Gantt view display Baseline 0 as default. If you want another Baseline to display, you will need to modify the desired view.

Updating an Existing Baseline or Capturing an Additional Baseline

1. Select the desired tasks (optional).
2. Click the **Project** tab.
3. Click the drop-down arrow on **Set Baseline** in the Schedule group.
4. Click **Set Baseline**.
5. Choose the desired options.
6. Click **OK**.

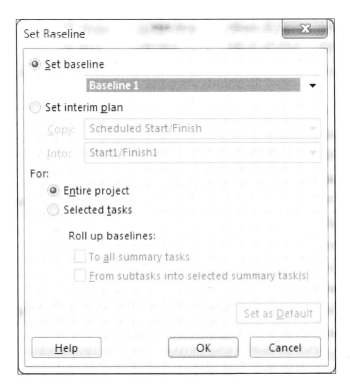

Figure 10-3   Set Baseline Dialog Box.

 Overwriting Baseline 0 will replace planned task information with current task information and eliminate all historical variance values. Be sure this is your intent before overwriting Baseline 0.

Overview of Tracking

As your project progresses, you should track the completion of tasks to determine if the tasks followed the expected schedule. You often have changes that occur once the project begins. You may, for example, have tasks that must be postponed, tasks that start early or late, or tasks that take longer than expected, so you should update your project often.

When the project is updated, you enter what actually happened. Items to be updated include when tasks start and finish, and how long tasks take to complete. You can also make any necessary changes to the schedule. The schedule is meant to guide you through the completion of the project, but it does not have to be inflexible. The schedule should change as necessary to reflect what is most likely to happen in the project.

There are many different ways to update the status of your project. For each task in your project, you can enter the actual start and finish dates, percent complete, actual duration, remaining duration, and so on, or you can have Project enter the information automatically.

If you enter the percent complete, actual duration, or remaining duration, Project calculates and updates the entries for the other fields. For example, if you specify that a two-day task is 50% complete, Project automatically transfers the current start date into the field for the actual start date, enters the actual duration as one day, and calculates the Cost and Work fields based on the task and resource information. You can change any of the information Project enters automatically.

When you update the information for subordinate tasks, Project automatically updates the summary task. You cannot update a summary task directly.

Tracking Activities With Project

Tracking is one of the simplest functions that you can perform in Project. Unfortunately, most managers have sub-optimized their plans by setting constraints, or they do not understand Effort Driven Scheduling and undermine the simple part of tracking actual progress.

Before you begin the mechanics of tracking, there are several things to consider that will affect the tracking process and how variances are calculated.

Setting the Status Date

When you update tasks, some of the automatic tracking features work based on the status date. For example, if uncompleted work on a task is rescheduled, Project uses the Status Date as the current point in time and therefore, the past is to the left of the status date and the future is to the right of the status date.

To set the status date, complete the following steps:

1. Click the **Project** tab.
2. Click date to the right of **Status Date** in the Status group.
3. Choose or type the desired date
4. Click **OK**.

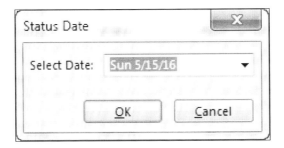

Figure 10-4   Status Date Dialog Box.

If you forget to set the Status Date, Project will use the Current Date for any features that typically require the Status Date, such as rescheduling a task and Earned Value calculations.

When you are ready to do the update for the next period, be sure to change the Status Date if you do not want Project to use the Current Date for this period. This is useful when you are a week behind in updating your schedule and you want it to reflect last week's progress.

Displaying the Tracking Gantt View

The Tracking Gantt view displays both the baseline and current Gantt bars for every task and is very useful when doing variance analysis.

To display Tracking Gantt Chart view:

1. Click the **Task** tab.
2. Click the drop-down arrow on **Gantt Chart** in the View group.
3. Click **Tracking Gantt**.

Figure 10-5   Gantt Chart Menu – Tracking Gantt Option.

This view uses the default Baseline fields. To display an alternate baseline such as Baseline1, the view will need to be customized.

Marking a Task by Percent Complete

This is the simplest task update method, but it is based on the assumption that you are able to determine what percent complete a task is and that the task is going according to schedule.

If you use this method, it is suggested that general benchmarks be established for what is meant by certain percent complete levels. For example, 25% complete means that work has actually started on the task. This will help avoid confusion and falling behind on tasks.

To update a task by percent complete:

1. Select the desired task(s).
2. Click the **Task** tab.
3. Click **Gantt Chart** in the View group (optional).
4. Click the desired percentage button in the Schedule group.

Figure 10-6   Project Ribbon – Schedule Group – Percent Complete.

This method may be useful to quickly update a large portion of the schedule and then you can go back and individually modify tasks that did not go according to schedule. Zero percent (0%) will essentially reset the task to incomplete.

Marking a Task on Track

Instead of choosing the percent complete, this method figures out the percent complete for you by marking the task complete to the status date (e.g., if the task should be done by the status date, the task will be marked

100% complete), but if only a portion of the task should be done by the status date, the percent complete will be calculated.

To mark a task on track:

1. Select the desired task(s).
2. Click **Mark on Track** in the Schedule group.

Figure 10-7   Project Ribbon – Schedule Group – Mark on Track.

Updating a Task That is Not on Schedule

When a task is not progressing as scheduled, you typically have information about what is occurring, such as a delayed start date, or an extended remaining duration. This method allows you to fill in the information you do have and remaining pieces will automatically calculate. For example, if you enter an actual Finish Date, Project will automatically record the task as 100% complete. If you enter 2 days of actual duration on a 5 day task, Project will automatically reduce remaining duration to 3 days.

To update a task that is not progressing according to schedule:

1. Select the desired task(s).
2. Click the drop-down arrow on **Mark on Track** in the Schedule group.
3. Click **Update Tasks**.
4. Choose or type the desired updates.
5. Click **OK**.

Figure 10-8   Project Ribbon – Schedule Group – Update Tasks.

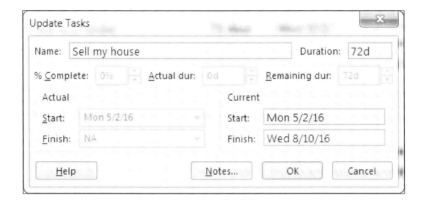

Figure 10-9   Update Tasks Dialog Box.

Suggestions:

- If the task has not started, but the duration is now going to take more or less time, simply adjust Remaining dur.
- If the task has started, but not on the planned date, enter the Actual Start.
- If the task is in progress, but the total duration is incorrect, enter both Actual dur and Remaining dur.
- If the task finished on a different date, simply enter Actual Finish. This will trigger 100 to be assigned to % Complete.

Although you can use this feature for multiple task updates, all the fields in the Update Tasks dialog box will display blank. Update tasks individually if you wish to see the current information about the task such as duration, and remaining duration.

Include notes to record the circumstances behind the update.
Notes are also a great way to document your schedule for others
to review.

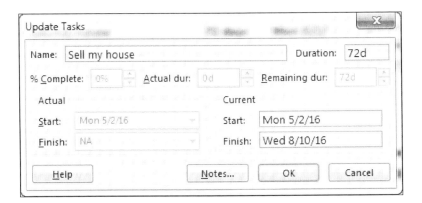

Figure 10-10 Update Tasks Dialog Box – Notes.

Rescheduling/Moving a Task

If you have not turned on calculation options as described later in this
chapter to automatically move a task, you may need to do that manually
to adjust the bars in the Tracking Gantt view so only uncompleted work is
shown in the future. When a task is moved, it can be moved either forward
or backward.

To reschedule/move a task:

1. Select the desired task(s).
2. Click the **Task** tab.
3. Click the drop-down arrow on **Move** in the Tasks group.
4. Click the desired option.

Figure 10-11   Project Ribbon – Task Group – Move.

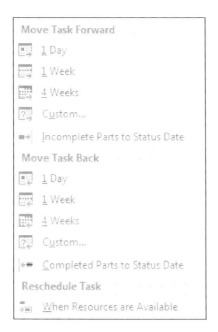

Figure 10-12   Move Task Menu.

Moving a task forward or backward puts a constraint on the task in its new location. Rescheduling a task postpones a task until resources are available, but does not put a constraint on the task.

Key Points to Remember

- The baseline is the original plan and is captured after the schedule is formally approved.
- Setting the baseline captures five fields: Start, Finish, Duration, Work and Cost.
- Changes can be incorporated into the baseline by overwriting selected tasks, resetting the existing baseline, setting a new baseline, or setting an interim plan.
- Baselines are required to display variances or to use earned value analysis.
- The Status Date defaults to the current date unless you modify it.
- Tracking Gantt view shows both baseline and current status of tasks.
- Percent complete tracking is the simplest but least accurate tracking method.
- Use Mark on Track when a task is progressing as scheduled.
- The Update Tasks feature is used when a task is not progressing as scheduled.
- During tracking you may need to postpone a task through the Move feature.

ADVISICON®

Chapter 11
Printing and Reporting

"All of man's artefacts,
whether hardware or software,
whether bulldozers or laws of
chemistry, are alike linguistic
in structure and intent."

~ Marshall McLuhan

Overview

The output from a schedule is important as a communication tool; therefore tailoring the view can be helpful to address the information needs of the audience. Views can be customized by formatting text, formatting bars, applying quick styles, and altering the general layout of the page. Printouts can be in Project file format, in PDF format, or image format. These options help you communicate with Project and non-Project users.

Besides a traditional view, reports can be created to communicate with others. Three popular report categories include Visual reports, Dashboard reports, and Timeline view reports. A Visual report exports information into Visio or Excel for further manipulation. A Dashboard report creates a visual output with blocks or sections of information such as graphs or tables. Dashboards may continue through multiple pages. A Timeline view report is designed for communication information at a high-level and it is easily transferred to other programs such as Word or Outlook. As you work with the individuals involved in your schedule, you will be able to determine the best output based on their needs.

Printing

Most of the print settings in Project 2013 are similar to other Microsoft Office products. Unique to Project 2013 is the ability to include project and task data in report titles using the header and footer options. We will also discuss printing Gantt charts on paper or using Gantt charts in presentations.

In this lesson, we will discuss:

- Print Settings
- Page Setup Options
- Copy Picture

Print Settings

Project 2013 gives you the ability to customize how a report will be printed. Seeing the final report before it is printed assures the user that they are printing the correct report in the format needed. Print options allow the user to select a printer and fine-tune which data will be printed. When the print options are selected, the current active project view will be printed.

To display print options :

- File → Print

To close print options:

- Click any tab above the ribbon bar

In *Table 11.1*, Gantt Chart is the active view. On the left side of the screen, several options are available:

Table 11.1   Print screen options

Option	Action and result
Print	Sends the report to the selected printer.
Copies	Determines the number of copies that will be printed.
Printer	Clicking the arrow on the right side of the box will open a drop-down menu and display all available printers.
Printer Properties	Clicking on the link will display additional printing properties.
Settings	Allows you to select which printer the image will be printed on.
Dates	Allows for selection of a date range for the printed report.
Pages	Allows for selection of specific page range.
Orientation	Landscape or Portrait.
Paper size choice	Select from a variety of paper sizes.
Page Setup	Dialog box that will allow for more customization choices.

Notice how the print screen maintains your options on the left and provides a preview of what the result will look like on the right. This gives you the flexibility to make changes before sending the schedule to the printer.

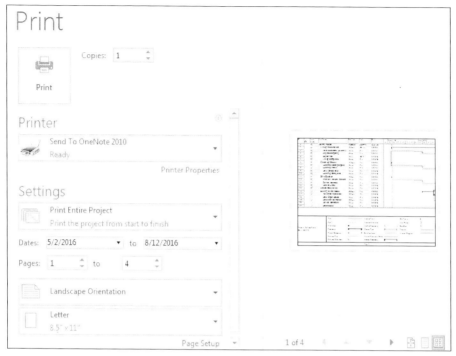

Figure 11-1   View of Printing options.

Click the down arrow on Settings to display more options to further refine the final printed report. These options are:

Table 11.2   Print Options from the File Tab

Option	Action and result
Print Entire Project	Default value. The entire project schedule will be printed using the current view.
Print Specific Dates	Only the data between the date range will be printed. This option is not available for all reports.
Print Specific Pages	Select specific page numbers to print.

Table 11.2   Print Options from the File Tab

Option	Action and result
Print Custom Dates and Pages	Date range and page number range will be printed.
Notes	Add the project notes to the printed report. Notes will be printed on a separate notes page.
All Sheet Columns	When selected, all columns within the current view will print.

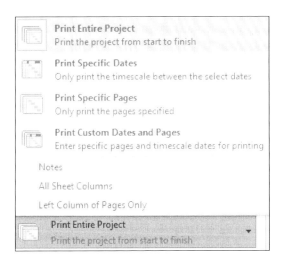

Figure 11-2   Print choices available when the Settings option is selected on the Print option screen.

Page orientation and paper size options are also available.

Viewing options to preview the final report are available by clicking on the buttons below the active project view in the lower right corner of the screen.

Table 11.3   Adjustment options available in the lower right corner of
              the Print options screen

Button	Represented by	Result
Left arrow	◀	Move one page to the left.
Up arrow	▲	Move one page up.
Down arrow	▼	Move one page down.
Right arrow	▶	Move one page to the right.
Actual size view		Actual size of printed report. Use sliders to see the entire page.
One page		Report will show one page at a time.
Multiple pages		Report will show in multiple page format.

Notice in this screen shot the preview options at the bottom. These are
often overlooked and will let you quickly preview another page or show
either a single page or all pages at once.

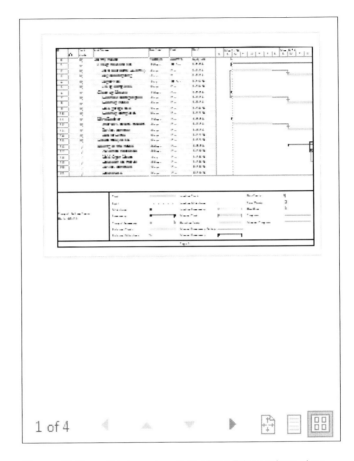

1 of 4

Figure 11-3   Print preview side of the Print options view.

Add the Print Preview button to the Quick Access Toolbar:

Click on the down arrow on the right side of the Quick Access toolbar

Select **Print Preview**

Figure 11-4   Add Print Preview to the Quick Launch Bar.

Page Setup Options

Page setup options are similar to options available in other Microsoft Office products. Project 2013 has some unique options specifically for the types of views available in the application. These unique options will be discussed in this lesson.

Project level data may be entered for project name, author, company, etc. and applied to the project header and footer information. This information is entered using the Advanced Properties dialog box. Once the data has been entered, the header and footer information is configured per report using the Page Setup options.

To add information in the Advanced Properties dialog box:

- File → Info → Project Information → Advanced Properties

The dialog box is shown below:

Figure 11-5   Advanced Properties box.

To display the Page Setup dialog box:

- File → Print → Page Setup

A dialog box will appear with the Page tab displayed. The options on this tab are similar to other Microsoft Office applications. The Margin tab contains the margin settings for the current report and an option to print borders around the data. Adjust these values as needed. The Header and Footer tabs allow for configuration of titles and footer information for reports. The view below shows the Header tab used for adding the project title values.

To add Header or Footer information to the title of a project:

- Click the **Header** or **Footer** tab.
- Click on the **Left**, **Center**, or **Right** tab in the lower section of the box.
- Click the down arrow to view the General drop-down menu.
- Select field value.
- Click **Add**.
- Repeat for additional data.

The Header and Footer settings are unique per report and should be checked using Print Preview before each reported is printed.

A current date is not preset to show in either the header or the footer title lines. Add the system's date using the center button above the General drop-down menu.

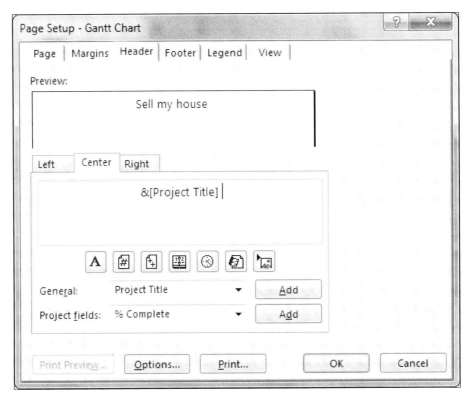

Figure 11-6   View of the Header tab in the Page Setup box.

The Legend tab is used to customize or turn off the legend printed on Gantt charts. If unique Gantt chart formatting has been created, the alternate color coding will automatically appear in the legend when the Gantt chart is printed. The Legend Labels button allows for font color and font selection changes. To disable the legend printed on Gantt charts, select None on the right side of the dialog box.

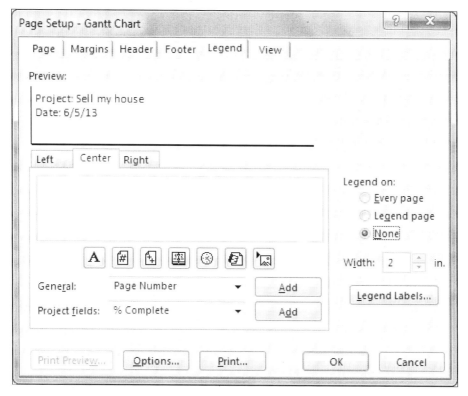

Figure 11-7   Page Setup box viewing the Legend tab.

The View tab contains options for specific views, but not all options will be available for each report. The options on the View tab are:

Table 11.4   Options available for Printing reports on the View tab of the Print Preview box

Option	Result of selecting option
Print all sheet columns	All columns in the table of the active view will be printed.

Table 11.4   Options available for Printing reports on the View tab of
the Print Preview box

Option	Result of selecting option
Print first (enter number) columns on all pages	Specify the number of columns to be printed on all pages of the report. When printing a Gantt chart, it is advantageous to add the task name to all pages. In Gantt Chart view, the first column of pages in your printout can be further refined by dragging the dividing bar which separates the entry table (left) and timescale (right) side.
Print notes	A separate notes page will be added to the report. Task ID numbers will be used to tie the note to the task.
Print blank pages	When printing Gantt charts, blank pages might result. Should these pages be printed?
Fit timescale to end of page	Adjusts the timescale for the report.
Print column totals	Adds totals to Resource Usage and Task Usage reports.
Print row totals for values within print date range	Adds totals to Resource Usage and Task Usage reports.

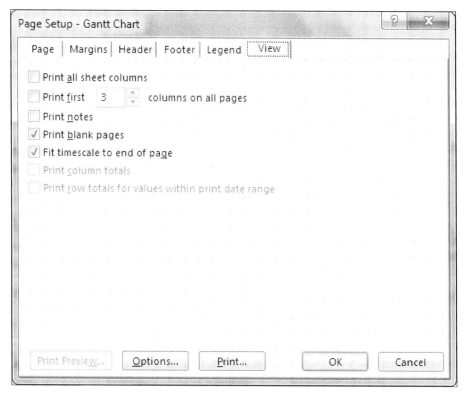

Figure 11-8   Page Setup box with View tab displayed.

Copy Picture

Use the Copy Picture tool to take a picture of your active view and store it on the clipboard. After it is stored, it can be pasted into PowerPoint, Word, Excel or any other application.

To use the Copy Picture tool, the view must be displayed and refined for the picture. Navigate to the view to be copied. Some adjustments to a view might include:

- Expand or collapse the work breakdown structure.
- Adjust timescale.
- Adjust titles in the timescale.
- Change formatting.
- Highlight tasks.
- Add drawing elements.

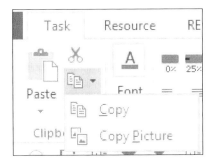

Figure 11-9   Copy Picture.

To use the Copy Picture tool:

- Click **Task** → down arrow to the right of the Copy Button → **Copy** Picture.

If printing a Gantt chart, adjust the vertical bar in the middle to show the columns to be included and click **Copy Picture** to open the Copy Picture dialog box shown below.

- **Render image** - select image to render For Screen, For Printer or To GIF image file.
- **Copy** - rows on screen or Selected rows.
- **Timescale** - as shown on the screen or date range.
- Click **OK** to copy to the clipboard.

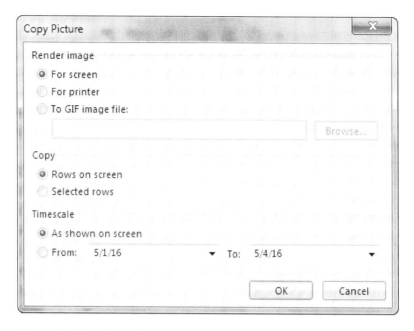

Figure 11-10   Copy Picture options box.

Use the image to paste into a Powerpoint presentation, a Word document, an email or other application. After pasting, resize the image as necessary.

Save as Project file in .PDF format

In Project 2013, we have the option to save project files as PDFs. Access to the option is located in the backstage view:

To create a .PDF file from the current view:

- File → Export → Create PDF/XPS Document → Create PDF/XPS

You will then be asked to select a location for the completed file. .PDF will be the default file type. Click on this value to change to .XPS files if necessary.

Click OK

Figure 11-11   Export file image as .PDF options.

You will then be given Document Export options to make some adjustments to the image:

- Publish Range: All or date range
- Include Non-Printing Information: Document Properties and Document Showing Markup
- PDF Options: ISO 19005-1 compliant (PDF/A)

Click OK to complete creating the .PDF image.

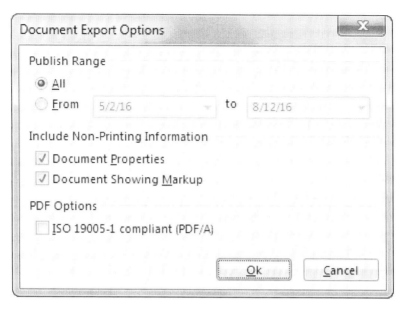

Figure 11-12   Create .PDF, Document export options.

The **Save As PDF** function is limited to a single-pane view (i.e.
without a split). If you have Gantt Chart with Timeline view displayed, the PDF will generate based on the currently selected
(active) pane. This will be either Gantt Chart or Timeline, not both.

Email a Project file as an Attachment

Another way to communicate project information is to email a copy of a project file to someone. The person who receives the file must have Microsoft Project 2010 or Microsoft Project 2013 to open the file.

To attach the open project file to an email:

File → Share → Email → Send as Attachment

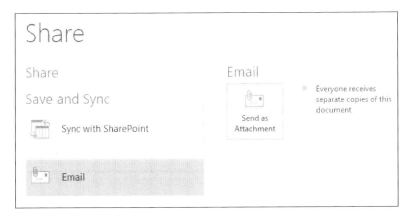

Figure 11-13   Share options in the backstage.

After clicking "Send as Attachment" Outlook will start, an email will be opened, the subject line will contain the name of the project and the file will be an attachment. Simply enter who the email should be sent to and add your comments. Click Send when you are ready to send the message.

Figure 11-14   Project file as an attachment in an email.

Refining Gantt Chart Formatting

The Gantt chart view may be altered as necessary to show the Gantt chart as needed for reports. Changes may be made to formatting, the time scale and data which is shown on the chart. In this section we will discuss these functions.

Using the Format Tab

The Format tab buttons help you customize the text, columns, colors, and other elements of each type of view. The groups and buttons in the Format tab are different for each type of view. If you are viewing a Gantt chart view you will receive a different set of options than you would if you were viewing the Resource Usage view. Below is a view of the Format ribbon when the Gantt chart view is displayed. The next two ribbon examples are the Format ribbon when viewing the Resource Usage view and the Team Planner view.

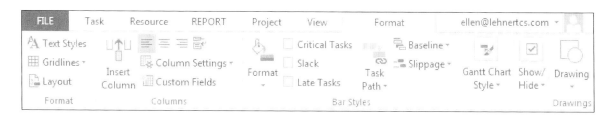

Figure 11-15   Project Ribbon – Gantt Chart Format Tab.

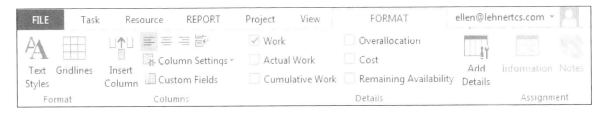

Figure 11-16   Project Ribbon – Resource Usage Format ribbon.

Figure 11-17   Project Ribbon – Team Planner Format tab.

Any Gantt chart may have changes made which will enhance the message you are trying to convey. For example, you can add the baseline or slack to the Gantt view. Right clicking on a Gantt bar and selecting Format Bar will allow you to change the color of a specific bar to quickly highlight specific tasks, or perhaps you want to add text to specific bars to help you identify them. Any changes that are made to a view will be held in the view and will be remembered the next time the view is displayed in the file.

Any changes you make to one Gantt Chart view do not change the look of other Gantt Chart views. For example, if you apply formatting to the Gantt Chart view, this will not carry over to the Detail Gantt view.

Formatting Text Styles

You can use text styles to change the format of text for one cell in a table or apply a unique format to an entire category of information, such as all critical tasks or all Milestone tasks. You may also want to change text to be more readable or to look distinct to garner attention for certain tasks.

You can format the text the same way for any view.

You can't format fonts in the Calendar view, but you can format categories of text, so text will have distinct formatting for items such as all critical tasks or all summary tasks.

Formatting Selected Text

To format selected text:

1. Select the cell(s) containing text that you want to format.
2. In the Ribbon, **Task** tab, **Font** group, click on the desired options or click on the dialog box launcher to display the **Font** dialog box.

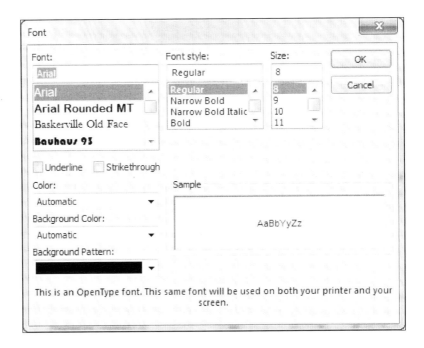

Figure 11-18   Text Styles Dialog.

3. From the three lists across the top of the dialog box you can select Font type, Font style and/or the Font Size. You can also select an Underline or Strikethrough check box and set the Font color, Background color and/or choose a Background pattern. A preview of your selection will appear in the sample area.
4. Click **OK** to save changes.

Formatting Categories of Text

To format categories of text:

1. In the Ribbon, **Format** tab, **Format** group click on **Text Styles**.
2. Click the drop-down arrow next to **Item to Change:** select a category of text.

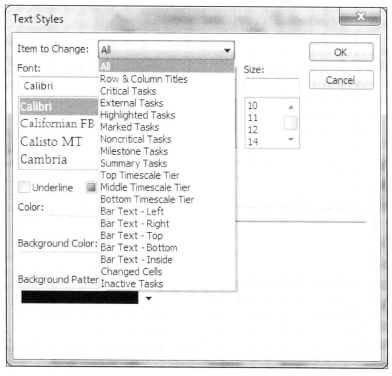

Figure 11-19   Text Styles Dialog with Items to Change Menu.

3. Select the settings that you want for the text, including font, font style, font size, color and script.
4. Click **OK** to apply the formatting.

Text Style formatting will only be applied to the view displayed when it is applied. It will not appear in other views. If the file is saved, the formatting will stay with the view.

Formatting the Gantt Chart

In addition to text styles you can format the task bars. You can make changes to the shape, color, and pattern, as well as style of the bar.

Changing the Gantt Bars Quickly Using a Style

With a single click, you can apply a pre-defined style to all bars in a Gantt Chart view.

To apply pre-defined styles to Gantt bars:

1. Apply a Gantt Chart view.
2. In the **Format** tab, **Gantt Chart Style** group, click a style in the **Gantt Chart Style** group.

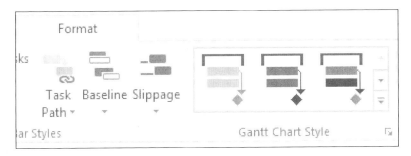

Figure 11-20   Gantt Chart Styles Group.

3. The style is instantly applied to all the bars in the view.

Changing the Color, Shape, or Pattern of Gantt Bars

To call attention to task bars in Gantt Chart view, you can change the color, shape, or pattern of individual task bars to separate them from other types of bars. This technique can be used to draw attention to task bars like milestones or summary tasks. Making changes using the Bar Styles box will change only the current view. All bars in the view such as Gantt bars, summaries or milestones will be affected by this change.

To format categories of task bars:

1. Apply a Gantt Chart view.
2. In the **Format** tab **Bar Styles** group, click the **Format** drop-down arrow, and click **Bar Styles**.

You can also double click within the chart portion of Gantt Chart view, but not on individual bars, to open the Bar Styles dialog box.

3. In the **Name** field, click the type of bar (such as Task or Progress) that you want to format.
4. Click the **Bars** tab at the bottom of the box.

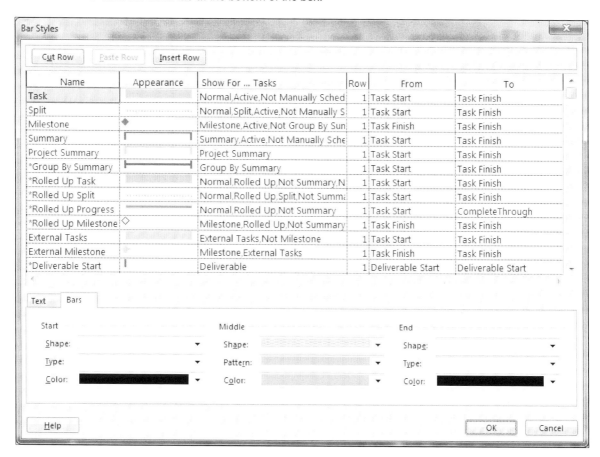

Figure 11-21   Bar Styles Dialog.

5. Under Start, Middle, and End, click the shapes, types or patterns, and colors for the bar.

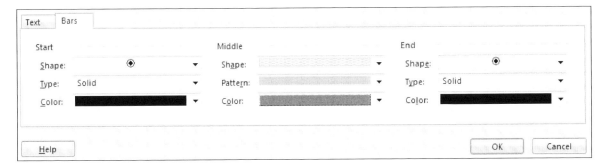

Figure 11-22   Bottom Pane of Bar Styles Dialog – Bars Tab Selected.

6. Click **OK** to save changes.

> To highlight a single Gantt bar by changing its formatting, right click on the individual bar and select **Format Bar**.

Changing the Appearance of Link Lines Between Gantt Bars

When you link tasks, Project displays link lines on a Gantt Chart view that show the dependency of the linked tasks.

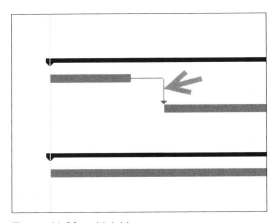

Figure 11-23   Link Line.

You can change the way link lines appear or hide the link lines.

To change the appearance of links between Gantt bars:

1. Apply a Gantt Chart view.
2. In the **Format** tab, **Format** group, click **Layout**.

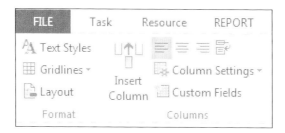

Figure 11-24   Format Tab, Format Section, Layout button.

3. Under **Links**, click the type of link line that you want to use. If you choose the first type of link, then the link lines will not appear.

Layout box options:

- **Links** - used to change the look of the link lines or turn them off.
- **Date format** - used to change the date format on the Gantt chart and will not affect the date shown in the tables.
- **Bar Height** - used to adjust the Gantt bars.
- **Always roll up Gantt bars** – used to roll up the Gantt bars when the outline level is collapsed, roll up the Gantt bars (example of rolled up bars is shown below).
- **Round bars to whole days** – used to make very short tasks more visible.
- **Show bar splits** - used when you have split tasks. Split tasks will also appear during tracking.
- **Show drawings** – drawing tools are located on the Format tab. Text boxes and arrows may be drawn on Gantt charts. Use this option to hide the drawings when needed.

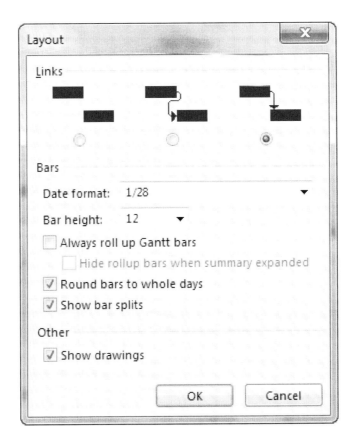

Figure 11-25 Layout Dialog Box.

Reporting

Communication is an essential part of project management. Project 2013 provides an abun-dance of textural and graphic reporting options to fulfill the communication requirements needed to help you manage your projects and communicate status to stakeholders.

In this lesson we will discuss:

- Visual reports
- Dashboard reports
- Timeline report

Visual Reports

Visual reports are graphical type reports that are available in Project 2013. These reports are defined using a template in Project 2013 and use either a Visio PivotDiagram or Excel PivotTable technology to generate the final report. Once a report is generated, changes and fine-tuning of the report can be performed through Visio or Excel.

Since Visual Reports use Pivot table technology, knowledge of Pivot tables is helpful for the project manager to gain the greatest benefit from these reports.

In this lesson we will discuss:

- Overview of Visual Reports
- The Anatomy of Pivot Tables
- Viewing a Visual Report
- Creating a Visual Report template

Overview of Visual Reports

Visual Reports are reports based on dimensions and measures that produce graphs using Pivot Tables. Pivot Tables will be discussed in the next lesson. When a Visual Report is run, an On-line Analytical Processing (OLAP) cube of data is built based on the metrics stated in the specifications for the Visual Report. After the cube is built, Project 2013 connects to either Visio or Excel to display the report. If an Excel-based report is selected, the report will be based on Pivot Tables. If a Visio-based report is selected, a Visio Pivot Diagram will be produced.

Once a report is generated, it can be manipulated as a Pivot Table and tailored to fit your needs. Types of manipulations include expanding and contracting outline levels, changing field values, selecting options, adding totals and changing the appearance of graphs. After the Visual Reports are generated, they can be saved or published to a reporting website.

Project 2013 provides multiple Visual Report definition templates found in the Visual Reports - Create Report dialog box. Options are available to filter the Excel templates from the Visio templates. All templates are contained in the All tab within the dialog box.

Sub tabs are provided for various report categories, and contain the following report options:

Table 11.5   Task Summary Tab

Report	Content	Excel or Visio
Critical Tasks status report (Metric)	Work and Work remaining for critical and non-critical tasks.	Visio
Critical Tasks status report (US)	Work and Work remaining for critical and non-critical tasks.	Visio

Table 11.6   Resource Summary Tab

Report	Content	Excel or Visio
Resource remaining work report	Work, Remaining Work, total Work for work resources.	Excel

Table 11.7   Assignment Summary Tab

Report	Content	Excel or Visio
Resource status report (Metric)	Work and Cost values per resource.	Visio
Resource status report (US)	Work and Cost values per resource.	Visio
Task status report (Metric)	Work and percent of work completed by WBS level.	Visio
Task status report (US)	Work and percent of work completed by WBS level.	Visio

Table 11.8   Task Usage Tab

Report	Content	Excel or Visio
Cash flow report	Timephased task cost data.	Excel

Table 11.9   Resource Usage Tab

Report	Content	Excel or Visio
Cash flow report (Metric)	Baseline Cost vs Actual Cost over time by resource type.	Visio
Cash flow report (US)	Baseline Cost vs Actual Cost over time by resource type.	Visio
Resource Availability report (Metric)	Total capacity, Work and remaining availability per. resource	Visio
Resource Availability report (US)	Total capacity, Work and remaining availability per resource.	Visio
Resource cost summary report	Resource costs per resource type.	Excel

Table 11.9   Resource Usage Tab

Report	Content	Excel or Visio
Resource work availability report	Work and remaining availability over time.	Excel
Resource work summary report	Work, Actual Work and Remaining Availability per resource.	Excel

Table 11.10   Assignment Usage Tab

Report	Content	Excel or Visio
Baseline Cost Report	Compares Baseline Cost, Actual Cost and Cost.	Excel
Baseline Report (Metric)	Baseline, Actual Work and Cost over time.	Visio
Baseline Report (US)	Baseline, Actual Work and Cost over time.	Visio
Baseline Work Report	Baseline Work, Baseline Cost, and Actual Work.	Excel

Table 11.10   Assignment Usage Tab

Report	Content	Excel or Visio
Budget Cost Report	Budget Cost, Baseline Cost, Cost and Actual Cost.	Excel
Budget Work Report	Budget Work, Baseline Work, Work, Actual Work.	Excel
Earned Value Over Time Report	Timephased – Actual Cost of Work performed, baseline values and Earned Value.	Excel

Anatomy of a Pivot Table

To understand Visual Reports, some understanding of Pivot Tables is helpful. Pivot Tables are flexible tables based on measures and dimensions. The information below is an overview of a Pivot Table based report. Additional information regarding Pivot Tables can be found in any Excel reference book, through software Help, or online.

In the table below, sales data from The Chocolate Company shows that sales of different prod-ucts have occurred in multiple locations. The Chocolate Company also keeps track of the cus-tomer type and products sold. We might want to know total sales by customer type, product or location. Pivot Tables have the flexibility to process any of these report requests quickly.

The data below is the source data that will be used to generate the Pivot Table:

Table 11.11   Sample data for Pivot table

Customer	Customer type	Location	Product	Quantity in bars	Price
Customer A	Retail	Chicago	Dark	48	120
Customer B	School	Rome	Milk	24	60
Customer C	Vending	Sydney	White	12	30
Customer D	Retail	Chicago	Dark almonds	36	45
Customer E	School	Rome	Milk almonds	48	120
Customer F	Vending	Sydney	White peanuts	24	60
Customer G	Retail	Chicago	Dark	12	30
Customer H	School	Rome	Milk	36	45
Customer I	Vending	Sydney	White	48	120
Customer J	Retail	Chicago	Dark almonds	24	60
Customer K	School	Rome	Milk almonds	12	30
Customer L	Vending	Sydney	White peanuts	36	45
Customer M	Retail	Chicago	Dark	48	120

In the view below, a Pivot Table has been created using the above data.

The data below is consolidated to show sales by Customer type:

Table 11.12   Pivot table generated in Excel
showing Customer type and
Sum of Price

Customer Type	Sum of Price
Retail	480
School	180
Vending	90
Wholesale	135
Grand Total	885

In the next example, the table was changed to show sales by Location:

Table 11.13   Pivot table generated in Excel
showing Location and Sum of
Price

Location	Sum of Price
Chicago	375
Rome	255
Sydney	255
Grand Total	885

In the next example, sales by Product:

Table 11.14   Pivot table generated in Excel showing Product and Sum of Price

Product	Sum of Price
Dark	270
Dark almonds	105
Milk	105
Milk almonds	150
White	150
White peanuts	105
Grand Total	885

Pivot Tables are easily changed to create the type of report necessary for your reporting needs, based on the values contained in the Pivot Table data. Visual Reports will be used to create the Pivot Diagram or Pivot Table but the project manager will need to customize the generated re-port.

Viewing Visual Reports

Project 2013 comes with built in Visual Report templates to report on cost, work and resource data. Having a specific goal in mind for the type of report you want will help generate more meaningful report data.

To open the Visual Reports – Create Report dialog box:

- Report → Visual Reports

To create a report:

- Select any report.
- Change timeframe (Days, Weeks, Months) for assignment (usage) data.
- Click **View**.

Figure 11-26   Visual Reports selection dialog box.

The report will generate by creating an OLAP cube and will open either Visio or Excel. In the generated Pivot Table select the data to be viewed on the report. Notice that the data viewed on the table can also be viewed in chart format.

Options are available for saving the generated OLAP cube or creating an Access database from the data by clicking the Save Data... button.

Visual report templates contain Microsoft Project Standard field
data. If customized field data was created, customized templates
can be created to contain the customized fields.

Dashboard Reports

What are Dashboard Reports?

Dashboard reports are reports that display project data is tabular and
graphic form. Each report displays different data and can be customized to
tailor the reports for each user's needs.

Introduction to Dashboards

Below is a view of the Overallocated Resources Dashboard Report. Note
that it contains two charts each representing different resource data. The
first chart represents Actual Work v Remaining Work. The second chart
displays resources that are Overallocated at the day level. Each of these
reports may be altered to adjust the chart type, chart elements and details
of the display data.

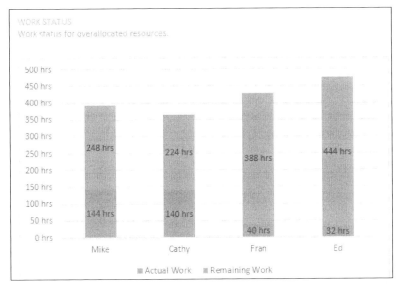

Figure 11-27   Dashboard Report – Actual Work Versus Remaining Work
Chart.

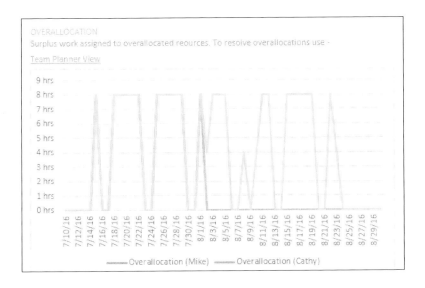

Figure 11-28   Dashboard Report – Overallocated Resources Chart.

Data included in the Dashboard Reports

Dashboard Reports contain data relating to project progress, variance calculations, and critical path. Below is some of the data which are included in the reports. If you are not using the data needed to populate the reports, the reports will not display properly.

Some of the data needed for the reports includes the following project data values:

- Task Duration, Cost and Work.
- Resource Cost and Work.
- Baseline comparison.
- Status date.
- Status field: Late, On Time, Future

To Display a Dashboard Report:

1. Click on the **Reports** tab.
2. Click on a Report Category: **Dashboards**, **Resources**, **Costs**, **In Progress**.

Figure 11-29   Ribbon bar for dashboard reports.

3. Click on a Report to display.

To change parameter values displayed on a Dashboard Report:

1. Click on the **Reports** tab
2. Click on a Report Category: **Dashboards**, **Resources**, **Costs**, **In Progress**

3. Click on a Report to display

4. Click inside of a graph. Options will appear on the right side of the view.

5. Change options as necessary. Close options by clicking on the X in the upper right corner of the options box.

6. Other changes may be made by clicking on formatting changes on the Design tab which will appear when a Report is selected.

Changes to Dashboard Reports will be remembered within the file and will appear the next time the report is viewed.

Clicking on the **Page Breaks** button will display the page breaks as they will occur when printing the report. The separate report graphics and tables may be dragged to different pages for printing purposes.

Timeline View Report

A timeline is a graphic that is usually displayed with long bars and key dates or date ranges. To create a high-level timeline report for an executive (or others who need to see a subset of your schedule), use Timeline view.

Customizing Timeline Views

The purpose of the Timeline view is to display project tasks using a timeline format and export the view to other applications such as Word, Excel, Outlook and Powerpoint.

Gantt Chart with Timeline is the default view in Project 2013. This view is a split screen with the Timeline view on the top and the Gantt Chart View on the bottom.

To turn Timeline view off/on:

- **Task → Gantt Chart**
- **View → Timeline**

Figure 11-30 Spit view section of the View ribbon.

Below is a view of the default Timeline view. The Timeline view is showing the information for the project summary task. The length of the timeline represents the duration of the project. There is a timeframe window open in the middle to highlight a specific timeframe:

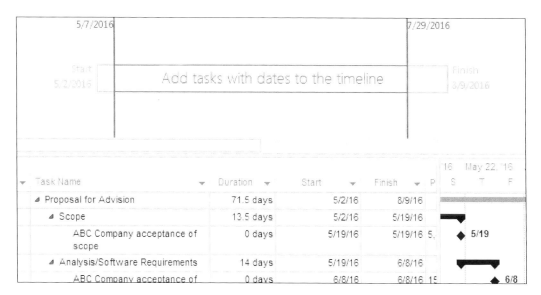

Figure 11-31 Default view of Timeline view.

To format or add more data to the Timeline view:

- Click inside the Timeline view window
- Click on the Format tab

Below is a view of the Timeline Format tab. Use the buttons on this bar to add additional tasks and format the Timeline view.

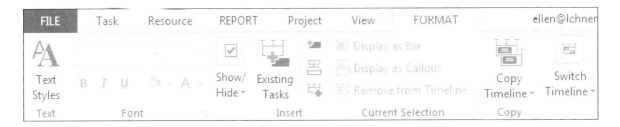

Figure 11-32 Format ribbon for Timeline View.

Within the Timeline view there is a timeframe window highlighted in the diagram below.

- The Timeframe window may be dragged left and right to emphasize different timeframes of the project schedule. The Gantt bars will adjust as the timeframe window is moved.
- Change the timeframe window by clicking in the timeline view and clicking the zoom slider in the lower right corner of the screen.
- The time density of the Timeline view does not have to match the time density of the Gantt Chart View.
- To turn on and off the Timeframe window, click the Pan & Zoom button on the Format bar.
- Use the Date format button on the Format bar to format the dates in the Timeline view.
- Use the Detailed Timeline button to show task names and dates in the view.

The view below shows the standard Timeline view with the Gantt chart view below:

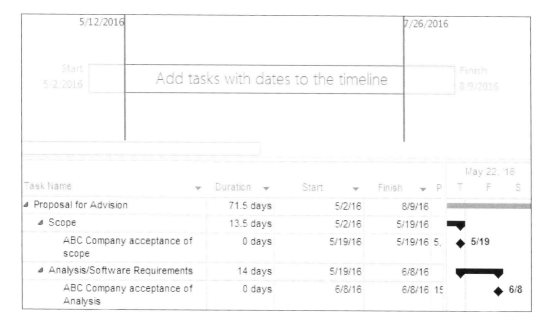

Figure 11-33   Timeline view with Gantt chart.

Adding additional tasks to the Timeline view will help build a better picture of your project. Tasks can be individually included to the Timeline view via the Task Information dialog box under the General tab. Double click a task to display the Task Information dialog box.

Figure 11-34   Task Information dialog box, General tab showing Display
on Timeline option.

The timeline format tab has several command buttons that will help flag
tasks for inclusion into the Timeline view. Clicking the Existing Tasks button
will display a list of all tasks for a project where you can scroll through and
select the tasks you want displayed in the Timeline view.

To add tasks to the timeline view using the Existing Tasks button:

- Click in the Timeline view.
- Click **Existing Tasks**.
- Using the check boxes, select the tasks to add.
- Click **OK** to close.

See below for an example of the Existing Tasks choice list. It is easy to tell
the difference be-tween summary and detail tasks:

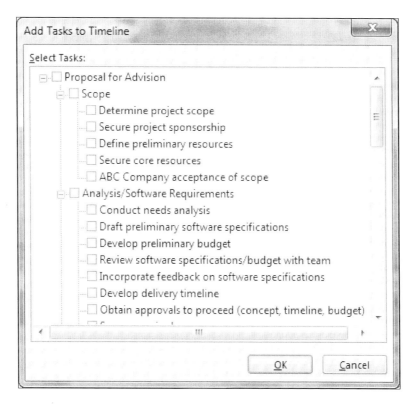

Figure 11-35   Add Tasks to Timeline dialog box.

The timeline view should be planned carefully to create a meaningful report. Too much information can confuse the reader. Consider creating a high level tasks report that shows summary sections of work within timeframes. Below is a view where outline Level 1 tasks have been added to the Timeline view.

To add Outline Level 1 tasks (Summaries) to the Timeline view:

- **Tasks → Gantt Chart**
- **View → Outline → Outline level 1**
- For each summary task to be added to the Timeline view, Select and Right click. Multiple selections may be made.
- Click **Add to timeline**

The Timeline view below, displays Outline Level 1 Summary tasks only and the Gantt chart display the same Outline Level 1 Summary tasks.

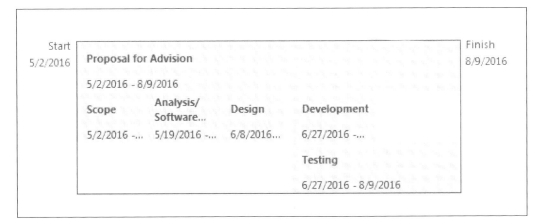

Figure 11-36   Timeline View Showing Outline Level 1 Summary Tasks.

Milestone and formatting for the bars can also be added to the Timeline view.

To add a milestone to the Timeline view:

- **Tasks → Gantt Chart**
- **View → Filter → Milestone**
- Select the milestone tasks and right click
- Click **Add to timeline**.

    To add formatting to the bars, click on the bar and click on a formatting tool in the Font section of the Ribbon.

The diagram below displays Outline Level 1 tasks with milestones added and formatting:

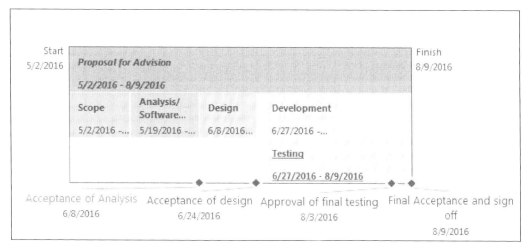

Figure 11-37   Timeline view with Summary tasks, formatting and milestones.

Tasks may be added to the project using the Timeline view Format tab. When adding tasks using these buttons, the tasks will be added to the end of the project schedule and will start on the first day of the project or the current date depending on the scheduling option. The choices are:

- Adding a new task to the timeline
- Adding a new callout task to the timeline
- Adding a new milestone to the timeline

Below is a view showing a new callout task and a new milestone added to the timeline and the project schedule. Callout tasks are originally placed above the timeline spanning the timeframe of the task. After they are created, they may be dragged to alternate locations within the Timeline View.

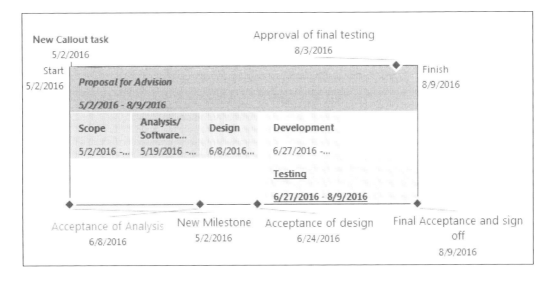

Figure 11-38   Timeline view with Call out task and added milestone.

To display an existing task as a callout task:

- Click on a task in the Timeline view
- Click **Display as a Callout**

To display a Callout task as a bar:

- Click on the Callout task
- Click **Display as Bar**

To remove tasks from the Timeline view using the Timeline Format tab:

- Click the task in the Timeline view
- Click **Remove from Timeline**

Tasks may be formatted and highlighted as necessary. Text styles and format buttons are available on the Timeline Format tab. Changing the colors of the timeline bars is helpful when highlighting information.

Too much information results in a hard to read Timeline view. Select what is important and what will convey your message. The view will become more meaningful and will result in a useful reporting tool. Typically Summary Tasks and Milestones are included in the Timeline view which would provide a high level report.

Exporting Timeline View

Timeline view is a great visual for executive summaries. To facilitate sharing information with executives, the Timeline may need to be exported to another application.

Timeline view must be displayed before you can export it to another application. The simplest method is to click the Timeline checkbox on the View tab. If this option is unavailable, you may need to uncheck the Details checkbox on the same tab.

To copy a timeline:

1. Click inside the Timeline view.
2. In the **Timeline Tools**, **Format** tab, click on **Copy Timeline** and choose the desired option.
   - **For e-mail** – Timeline size is reduced to fit into an Outlook message. Small size.
   - **For presentation** – Optimized for a PowerPoint presentation. Medium size.
   - **Full Size** – Uses the full size of the timeline as displayed in Project. Large size.

You can paste in Outlook to email it to peers or in PowerPoint to format it further.

Figure 11-39   Copy timeline options.

You can also save the Timeline as an Adobe Acrobat file using the File, Export, Create PDF/XPS Document option.

Key Points to Remember

- Projects can be saved in PDF format to e-mail to others without access to Project or when you want to ensure the data does not change.
- Print and Page Setup options can be tailored to alter the layout of printouts or PDF files.
- Use Text Styles to format a specific type of task globally.
- Gantt Chart Styles globally change the display of the Gantt bars.
- Use Bar Styles to format a specific type of Gantt bar globally.
- Use Layout to modify the link line appearance.
- Visual reports extract data into either Visio PivotDiagrams or Excel PivotTables where they can be modified further.
- Dashboard reports include graphical and tabular components and are very visual ways of representing scheduling information.
- Use Timeline view to create a graphical executive summary of your schedule.

Appendix A
Project Feature Coverage

Which Project Client Should I Use?

Microsoft Project comes in three different desktop clients (Project Profes sional, Project Professional for Office 365, and Project Standard), and two supporting clients: PWA for web browser-based interaction, and Project Lite for tablet-based interaction.

Each of these different versions of the Project client offer a unique set of feature coverage. We've grouped Project's features into the following feature sets:

- Anywhere Access
- Work Management
- Demand Management
- Portfolio Analytics & Selection
- Resource Management
- Schedule Management
- Financial Management
- Task & Timesheet Reporting
- Collaboration
- Issue & Risk Management
- Reporting & Business Intelligence
- Program Management
- Governance

Use this guide to determine the Project client(s) you'll need to bring your programs, portfolios, and projects to completion.

| Professional | Pro for 365 | Standard | PWA | Lite |

Professional

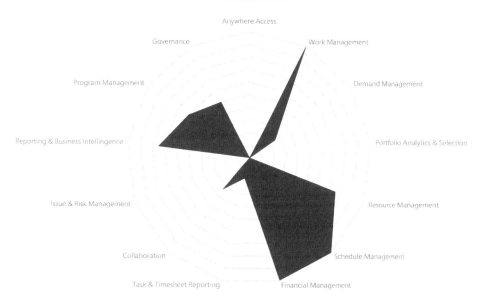

Pro for 365

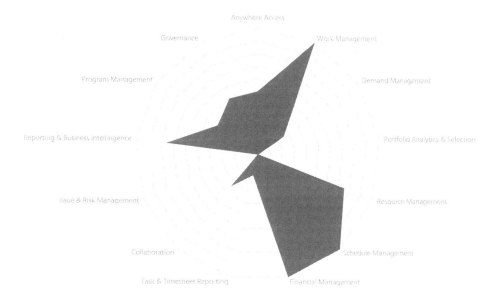

Standard

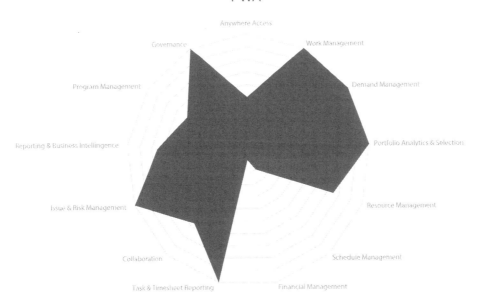

PWA

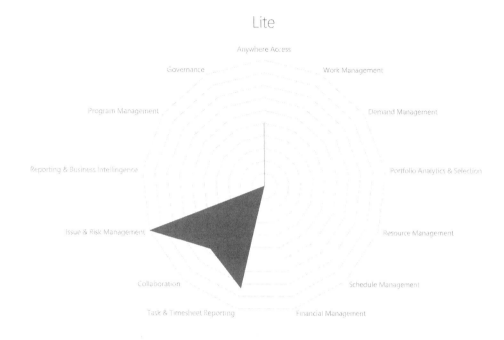

Lite

Appendix B

Advisicon Services and Training

About Advisicon

Advisicon delivers strategic project control solutions using advanced project and portfolio management methodologies, custom application development and consultative training.

Our clients throughout North America and Latin America have realized quantifiable results through our unique approach of combining knowledge transfer, optimization and sustainability of processes and technology while increasing stakeholder competencies.

Consulting and Training Services

- SharePoint & business intelligence training & consulting
- Project, program and portfolio methodology & technology training
- Project management office & Program management organizational maturity consulting
- Lifecycle management; organizational change and productivity solutions with integration consulting
- Assessments and optimization consulting for project and work management
- Microsoft® Project, and Project Server solution and integration consulting (all versions)
- Microsoft® SharePoint Services and Server solution and integration consulting (all versions)
- Dynamic project scheduling, program administration and staffing services and consulting
- Proprietary consultative technology and methodology training curriculum (public and customized)
- Business process and ERP system integration solutions and consulting (e.g. SAP, Dynamics, Lotus, IBM, Oracle)
- Custom application development (complex databases, integrations, reports, workflows and dashboards)

Microsoft Gold Certified Partner

Advisicon is Microsoft Gold Certified Project and Portfolio Management Partner – Microsoft's highest partner ranking with competencies in Collaboration and Content and Learning.

Project Management Institute Global Registered Education Provider (REP)

Advisicon is a Global Registered Education Provider (REP) of the Project Management Institute (PMI). Our clients have confidence knowing that they have chosen an organization that is qualified to provide the highest level of project management training, and the convenience of receiving Professional Development Units (PDUs).

Knowledge Transfer

Advisicon consultants first learn the key business drivers to any successful solution. Simultaneously, Advisicon consultants teach clients to internalize and standardize project management best practices and use of technology. Clients receive task-specific coaching, in-depth process development, customized project management methodology and supervised training with the technology.

Optimization

Advisicon consultants integrate project management best practices and project management technologies to fit each client's organizational structure, strategy, goals and culture.

Sustained Results

Through Advisicon's phased approach, our clients are able to adopt and implement strategic project management improvements one step at a time, growing from one level of project management maturity to the next. Through this process of optimization and knowledge transfer, Advisicon clients realize sustained results and scalable business options.

Training Programs

Advisicon offers courses in both methodology and technology. Our methodology courses cover project management best practices, while our technology courses teach the implementation of project management best practices with Microsoft tools.

Advisicon Project Management Courses

Practical Project Management

Learn how to manage projects from initiation to close-out. This practical course teaches participants how to successfully initiate, plan, execute, control and close-out projects applying industry best practices. Students will learn project management concepts, helpful standard terminology, and established methods based on the Project Management Institute (PMI®) Project Management Body of Knowledge (PMBOK®).

Mastering Requirements Gathering

Learn how to gather and manage project requirements successfully. This course teaches participants how to elicit, characterize, document, analyze, validate, verify and manage requirements for new projects, products and services. Participants will learn how to define and document high-level business requirements, identify user classes & representatives, select elicitation techniques, differentiate and prioritize functional & non-functional

requirements from users, identify business rules, and review and verify requirements with stakeholders.

Advisicon Technology Courses

Managing Projects with Microsoft Project

Learn how to use Microsoft Project to build, optimize and manage project schedules. This course teaches participants how to use Microsoft Project to successfully create, track, manage and modify project schedules and resource pools. Participants will learn how to apply best practices, tips and tricks to planning and managing projects with Project.

Microsoft Project Server for Administrators

Learn how to configure, customize, administer and support Microsoft Project Server. Administrators will learn how to configure, customize and support Project Server. This course trains participants to set up and support enterprise-wide project management standards, templates, resource pools, custom fields, management metrics and reporting, as well as how to manage Project Web App.

Microsoft Project Server for Project Managers

Learn how to build, publish, and manage project schedules, issues, risks, deliverables, resources, and documents across an enterprise with Microsoft Project Server. Project Managers will learn to build, track and manage project schedules with Microsoft Project Professional and publish them to Project Server, and how to track, analyze, and report on projects through Project Web App.

Microsoft Project Server for Team Members

Learn how to use Microsoft Project Server to contribute to projects across an enterprise. This course trains participants how to update and manage project tasks, enter and report on risks, issues, documents and new tasks through Project Web App.

Using SharePoint for Effective Project Management

Learn to use Microsoft SharePoint to manage project team collaborate on projects. This course teaches participants how to design, create customize and use SharePoint to collaborate, share documents, communicate and coordinate project activities, deliverables, communications, risks, and issues.

Advisicon Flowcharts

Advisicon has created a very practical set of project management flow-charts to help project managers, PMOs, and project team members plan, collaborate, and track project activities more effectively.

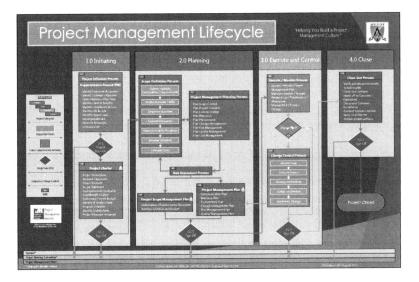

Figure B-1   Project Management lifecycle.

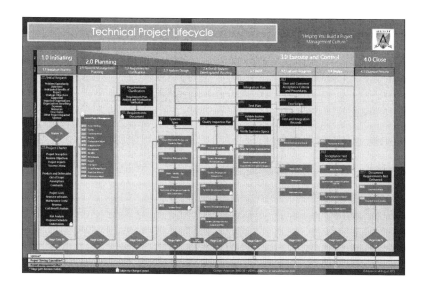

Figure B-2   Technical Project lifecycle.

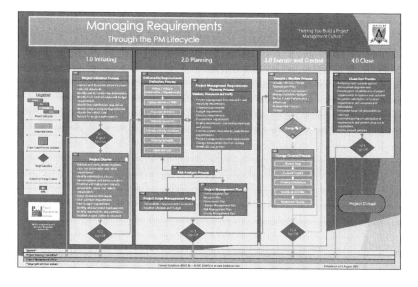

Figure B-3   Managing Requirements throughout the Project Management Lifecycle.

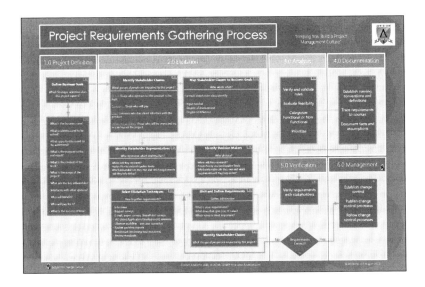

Figure B-4   Project Requirements Gathering Process.

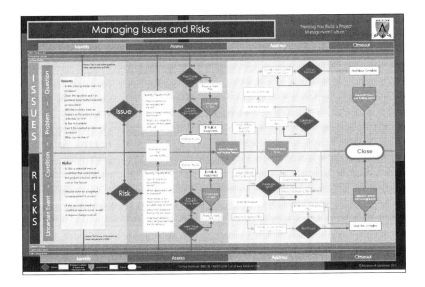

Figure B-5   Managing Issues and Risks.

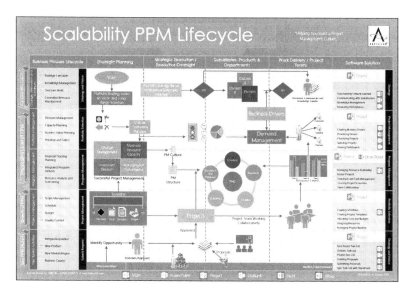

Figure B-6   PPM Lifecycle.

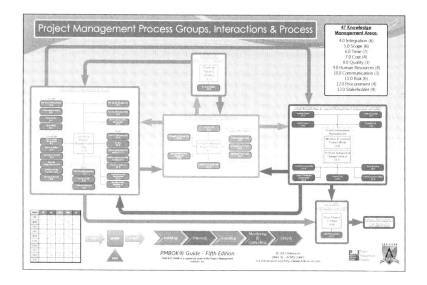

Figure B-7   Project Management Process Groups, Interactions & Process.

Advisicon Project Management Tools

Advisicon has created several project management tools to help project managers, PMOs, and project teams standardize and apply project management best practices. These tools will provide valuable project insight and analysis and save you days and weeks of work. You don't need to reinvent the wheel! Get the tools you need to manage your projects more effectively today!

RACI Charts, Project Risk Register, Stakeholder Support Analyzer, and Risk Analyzer are just some of the tools we offer.

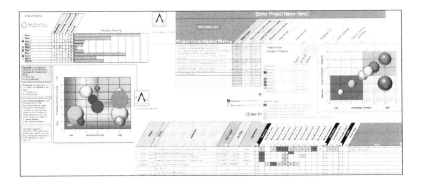

Optimization, Knowledge Transfer, and Sustained Results

www.Advisicon.com

Web Store: http://store.advisicon.com

email: Info@Advisicon.com

Toll free: 1.866.362.3847